Small Enterprises and Economic Development

Micro and small enterprises (MSEs) have been recognized as a major contemporary source of employment and income in a growing number of developing countries, yet relatively little is known about the characteristics and patterns of change in these enterprises. This volume examines the dynamics of MSEs in the development process. Drawing on a unique set of surveys conducted in twelve countries in Africa and Latin America, the authors map the patterns of change in MSEs in the developing world.

Subjects covered include:

- significance of new start and closure rates of MSEs;
- factors involved in expansion rates and growth patterns of MSEs;
- the role of gender in MSEs evolution.

Small Enterprises and Economic Development also develops a four-fold characterization of MSEs, from which follows an original reflection on the problems faced by and the diverse needs of MSEs. The authors conclude by drawing important lessons for donors and implementing agencies, based on the need to tailor policy to the varying contributions to development and needs of different MSEs. Reader-friendly in its presentation of a multitude of real-life examples and insightful in its suggestions for improving development assistance efforts, this volume will be welcomed by students and researchers in development economics and studies, as well as all interested policy-makers.

Carl Liedholm is Professor of Economics at Michigan State University. He has written widely in the field of economic development. **Donald C. Mead** is Professor of Agricultural Economics at Michigan State University. He has published widely on MSEs in developing countries.

Routledge Studies in Development Economics

1 Economic Development in the Middle East
Rodney Wilson

2 Monetary and Financial Policies in Developing Countries
Growth and stabilization
Akhtar Hossain and Anis Chowdhury

3 New Directions in Development Economics
Growth, environmental concerns and government in the 1990s
Edited by Mats Lundahl and Benno J. Ndulu

4 Financial Liberalization and Investment
Kanhaya L. Gupta and Robert Lensink

5 Liberalization in the Developing World
Institutional and economic changes in Latin America, Africa and Asia
Edited by Alex E. Fernández Jilberto and André Mommen

6 Financial Development and Economic Growth
Theory and experiences from developing countries
Edited by Niels Hermes and Robert Lensink

7 The South African Economy
Macroeconomic prospects for the medium term
Finn Tarp and Peter Brixen

8 Public Sector Pay and Adjustment
Lessons from five countries
Edited by Christopher Colclough

9 Europe and Economic Reform in Africa
Structural adjustment and economic diplomacy
Obed O. Mailafia

10 Post-apartheid Southern Africa
Economic challenges and policies for the future
Edited by Lennart Petersson

11 Financial Integration and Development
Liberalization and reform in sub-Saharan Africa
Ernest Aryeetey and Machiko Nissanke

12 Regionalization and Globalization in the Modern World Economy
Perspectives on the Third World and transitional economies
Edited by Alex F. Fernández Jilberto and André Mommen

13 The African Economy
Policy, institutions and the future
Steve Kayizzi-Mugerwa

14 Recovery from Armed Conflict in Developing Countries
Edited by Geoff Harris

15 Small Enterprises and Economic Development
The dynamics of micro and small enterprises
Carl Liedholm and Donald C. Mead

Small Enterprises and Economic Development

The dynamics of micro and small enterprises

Carl Liedholm
and Donald C. Mead

ROUTLEDGE

London and New York

First published 1999
by Routledge
11 New Fetter Lane, London EC4P 4EE

Simultaneously published in the USA and Canada
by Routledge
29 West 35th Street, New York, NY 10001

Typeset in Goudy by Routledge
Printed and bound in Great Britain by
Mackays of Chatham PLC, Chatham, Kent

British Library Cataloguing in Publication Data
A catalogue record for this book is available from the British Library

Library of Congress Cataloging in Publication Data
Liedholm, Carl. Small enterprises and economic development: the dynamics of micro and small enterprises / Carl Liedholm and Donald C. Mead.
p. cm.
Report on work of the Growth and Equity through Microenterprise Investments and Institutions (GEMINI) Project, primarily supported by U.S.A.I.D.
Includes bibliographical references.
1. Small business. 2. Economic development. I. Mead, Donald C. II. Title.
HD2341.L53 1998
338.64'2–dc21 98–34289 CIP

ISBN 0–415–19351–6 (hbk)

Contents

Tables

Acknowledgments

The work reported upon in this book was primarily supported by the US Agency for International Development, in core funding and buy-ins to the Growth and Equity through Microenterprise Investments and Institutions (GEMINI) Project, Contract No. DHR-5448-C-00–9080–01. Special thanks go to Elisabeth Rhyne, Project Monitor for the GEMINI Project through most of its life, for her support and encouragement.

Equally important has been the support from our GEMINI colleagues. Joan Parker, Matthew Gamser, Maria Otero, Kathy Stearns, Larry Reed, Jim Boomgard, and Mohini Malhotra deserve special mention.

A third group to whom we are indebted includes those who supervised the field surveys and undertook analyses of individual countries. Particular thanks go to Miguel Cabal, Lisa Daniels, Yacob Fisseha, Todd Gustafson, Michael McPherson, and Joan Parker. We have learned much from each of them.

1 Introduction

Micro and small enterprises (MSEs) are a major feature of the economic landscape in all developing countries today. The contribution of these enterprises to the creation of jobs and to the alleviation of poverty has been recognized by many Third World governments. They have been given prominence in many development plans as well as in the strategies of many donors.

In most developing countries, the contribution of MSEs to employment and income appears to have been increasing over time. To some observers, this is an encouraging sign: markets are working, people are finding opportunities to participate in ways that empower and nourish many people, particularly including those that are otherwise most disadvantaged. To other observers, however, this increase in the numbers of people engaged in MSEs is a sign of failure of the economy to provide productive jobs; people are forced to take refuge in activities that provide only minimal subsistence support.

Sorting out these differences is of great importance to those who wish to address the problem of poverty in the developing world. It is important to understand the characteristics and patterns of the changes that are taking place in the domain of MSEs, combining this with a vision of how things might develop better in the future in order to specify things that might be done to help bring about that preferred outcome. An important part of this sorting out involves a better understanding of the growth process among MSEs.

Most past research in this area, however, has been static in its orientation, providing a picture of how things look "today" (i.e. as of the time of the study). What kind of static picture emerges from the findings of these studies?

MSE characteristics: a snapshot

The overall profile of MSEs provides the context for examining dynamic issues. Since many aspects of this structure have by now become familiar, this review can be brief, highlighting aspects that are relevant to the discussion of enterprise dynamics that is the central focus of this volume.[1]

Magnitude

The findings from house-to-house visits that probe for the existence of MSEs make clear that the number of such enterprises is far larger than what is reported in most official statistics. The latter often cover only firms that are registered or in other ways recognized by the authorities; it is clear that large numbers of the smallest enterprise escape the attention of the administration, either because they seek to remain hidden, because they are excluded from the registration requirements, or because officials do not have the staff or the inclination to pursue those that do not register. Survey results in a number of countries have found that 17–27 percent of the population of working age are employed in MSEs (see Table 1.1 for all the aspects of this static profile). Employment densities – the number of people engaged in MSE activities per 1,000 persons in the population – ranged from 70 to 90 in Botswana, Kenya, Lesotho, and Malawi to well over 100 in the Dominican Republic, Swaziland, and Zimbabwe. In five of the African countries with the most comprehensive surveys, the estimated total number of people engaged in MSEs is nearly twice the level of employment in registered, large-scale enterprises and in the public sector.[2]

Size distribution of MSEs

The majority of activities categorized as MSEs are very small; most consist of only one person working alone. Self-employment is thus a central characteristic of the MSE world. If one defines the MSE universe as being made up of those firms with 1–50 workers, the larger end of the tail – those with ten or more workers – constitute less than 2 percent of the businesses in virtually all the countries in Africa covered by the surveys. The Dominican Republic stands out in this regard, with its substantially smaller share of one-person enterprises and much larger numbers at the upper end of the small-enterprise spectrum.[3]

Table 1.1 Characteristics of microenterprises

	Botswana	*Kenya*	*Lesotho*	*Malawi*	*Swaziland*	*Zimbabwe*	*South Africa**	*Dominican Republic*
MSE employment/population age 15–64 (%)	17	18	17	23	26	27	NAv	19
MSE employment per 1,000 persons in the population	71	83	84	92	118	127	81	109
Share of all MSEs that are one-person enterprises (%)	65	47	79	61	69	69	47	22
Share of all MSEs with 10–50 workers (%)	3	2	1	1	2	2	1	18
Share of hired workers (%)	39	24	10	18	15	16	19	36
Locational breakdown of MSE employment (%)								
Urban areas	24	15	18	12	25	30	NAp	46
Rural towns	28	7	10	4	10	6	NAp	18
Rural areas	48	78	72	84	65	64	NAp	36
Sectoral breakdown of enterprises: urban areas only (%)								
Manufacturing	15	18	35	29	33	64	17	21
Commerce	71	74	41	62	56	30	70	63
Sectoral breakdown of enterprises: rural areas only (%)								
Manufacturing	34	27	62	36	70	75	NAp	15
Commerce	64	66	27	60	24	16	NAp	75
Share of enterprises owned by females (%)	75	46	73	46	84	66	62	46
Share of all workers that are females (%)	67	40	76	40	78	57	78	38

Source: Survey data (see Bibliography) except for the population data in the first line, which are taken from United Nations and World Bank statistics. Note that, in the sectoral breakdown, the remainder of the enterprises are in services. NAv = Not Available; NAp = Not Applicable.
*Includes two townships only.

Labor force characteristics

Since most MSEs operate as one-person enterprises, it is not surprising that the largest single employment category is working proprietors, a group that comprises more than half the MSE work force in most countries. When unpaid family members are added, one finds that, in most countries, working owners and their family members, unpaid but active in the enterprise, comprise about three-fourths of the MSE labor force. Only in a few countries do hired workers comprise as much as 20 percent of the MSE labor force. Botswana and the Dominican Republic stand out in this regard: in those countries, over a third of the labor force is made up of hired workers. Trainees and apprentices add a significant share of workers in some locations, particularly in West Africa; in Southern Africa, as in other parts of the Third World, the survey results indicate that apprentices comprise less than 10 percent of the MSE labor force.

Location

One important finding from the surveys is that, in each of the countries studied, the majority of MSEs operate in rural areas. The share of all enterprises in urban locations – those cities and towns with at least 20,000 inhabitants – reached as high as 46 percent in the Dominican Republic and 30 percent in Zimbabwe, but it was 25 percent or less in all the other countries. Even adding in enterprises in rural towns – those concentrations with 2,000–20,000 persons – still generally left well over half of all enterprises in rural areas in most countries.

Composition of activities

It is typically believed that MSEs are primarily hawkers and small traders. There is some truth to this perception, since in several countries the majority of enterprises are engaged in commerce. It is important to note, however, that, in all countries, small manufacturing firms engaged in transformation activities are also an important component of the MSE sector. Manufacturing activities are particularly significant in rural areas; in fact, in each of the African countries with the relevant data, manufacturing enterprises constitute a substantially higher share of MSEs in rural than in urban areas. Only in the Dominican Republic was manufacturing more prevalent among urban enterprises.

Among manufacturing MSEs, the surveys have consistently found three types of activities to be the most important categories: textiles and wearing apparel, food and beverages, and wood and forest products. These three sectors contribute about 75 percent of small manufacturing enterprises in urban areas, and nearly 90 percent of manufacturing enterprises in rural areas. Yet these apparent regularities hide substantial variations from country to country and between urban and rural areas within one country as to which activity is most prevalent, as well as the nature of the dominant activities within each of these three broadly defined sectoral groupings. These country-specific differences appear to reflect differing raw material endowments (e.g. the availability of wood for furniture, of maize, millet or bananas for beer, or of cotton for weaving and dressmaking), as well as tastes and consumption patterns of people in different locations.

Gender

The majority of MSEs in most countries are owned and operated by women. In addition, since working proprietors are the single largest category of the labor force, the great majority of workers are also women. MSEs headed by women tend to be concentrated in a relatively narrow range of activities: beer brewing, knitting, dressmaking, crocheting, cane work, and retail trade. MSEs headed by women are more likely than their male counterparts to operate from the home. Since it is the home-based MSEs that tend to be overlooked, both in assistance projects and in official statistics, women owners of MSEs are particularly likely to be "invisible entrepreneurs."

Efficiency

Turning to static measures of economic efficiency, earlier studies based on an analysis of detailed data on production costs in four developing countries suggest substantial differences in economic efficiency by enterprise size. In particular, the data indicate that net returns per hour of family labor are significantly higher for enterprises with 2–5 workers, compared to those enterprises with only one self-employed person working alone.[4] This increase in economic efficiency continues for the next higher size category, those with 6–9 workers; thereafter, the number of observations in these data is small and the results more ambiguous. Similar results were found in a recent survey of MSEs in Kenya.[5] In all of these studies, the data suggest that one-person enterprises generate the lowest net returns; even a small increase in size is associated with significant increases in economic efficiency, which for these small establishments is closely associated with the levels of income earned by those working in the enterprise.

Methodological approaches to the study of enterprise dynamics

A comparison of snapshot pictures based on one-time surveys in countries at different levels of development and with different policy settings, combined with historical data in a few countries (usually, today's industrialized countries), has led to some important generalizations concerning patterns of growth of MSEs. There is a major limitation on these cross-sectional and historical time series studies, however: their orientation has been, of necessity, almost entirely macroeconomic, focusing on the changing share of total output, income and employment in enterprises of different types and sizes. While these studies have enabled us to understand some important aspects of the evolving role of MSEs in the macroeconomy, they have been able to shed much less light on the microeconomics of change – patterns by which individual enterprises are started, evolve, and perhaps eventually go out of business.

In the past five years, a number of new studies have been undertaken that have helped to change that situation. These studies have used new survey techniques that make it possible to be more precise about patterns of enterprise births, survival, growth, and closure. Among the data collection innovations have been the introduction of "closed" MSE surveys; repeated panel surveys of MSEs; "tracer" studies of MSEs that had existed in the past; and modified baseline surveys that generate information about past patterns of growth since MSE start-up.

These new surveys, which were undertaken as part of the GEMINI project funded by USAID and undertaken under the supervision of staff from Michigan State University, have been conducted in twelve countries. The most comprehensive MSE growth data were generated in six core countries: Botswana, Kenya, Malawi, Swaziland, Zimbabwe, and the Dominican Republic. In each of these countries, not only was the modified baseline survey administered nationwide, but at least one other dynamic survey was also administered. Less comprehensive information was generated from six other countries: Guinea, Jamaica, Lesotho, Niger, Nigeria, and South Africa. More details concerning the countries and surveys, which were administered to over 65,000 MSEs, are provided in Chapter 2.

These surveys provide rich new insights into patterns of enterprise dynamics at the level of the individual producing unit. This book summarizes what has been learned from these studies.

The universe of enterprises covered in the surveys includes all enterprises engaged in non-primary activities (i.e. excluding agriculture, forestry, hunting and fishing, mining and quarrying, but including the transformation, transport and marketing of primary products), where at least 50 percent of the output is sold (i.e. excluding products made primarily for home consumption), and engaging up to fifty workers (including unpaid family members, working proprietors, apprentices and part-time workers). Our definition of MSEs thus encompasses establishments consisting of one person weaving baskets for sale in the market; it also includes factories with forty or fifty workers, using complex machinery. We refer to this total as micro and small enterprises (MSEs). For some purposes, our focus is on the smaller end of this range, those with ten or fewer workers, referred to as microenterprises.

The contribution of MSEs to development

Why are such enterprises worthy of study? MSEs have the potential to contribute in a number of important ways to the development process. Among the most significant of these are the following:

1 contribution to household income and welfare:

  (a) providing income maintenance for those with few options;
  (b) providing a basis for growth in income and welfare through asset accumulation, skill development, and access to more rewarding economic opportunities;
  (c) providing employment;

2 contribution to self-confidence and empowerment of the individual:

  (a) recognition of the dignity of the individual;
  (b) spreading the vision that change is possible;

3 contribution to social change, political stability, and democracy:

  (a) through increasing confidence in local, representative, community-based institutions;
  (b) through the development of individual feelings of responsibility and participation in governance;
  (c) through the creation of institutional structures reflecting people's needs and objectives;

4 contribution to distributional or developmental objectives:

  (a) providing new opportunities for the poor;
  (b) providing new opportunities for women;
  (c) providing new opportunities for those in rural areas, and in isolated locations;

5 contributions in the area of demographic change:

(a) through reduction in birth rates;
(b) through reduction in rural–urban migration.

It is obvious that many of these are closely interrelated or overlapping. The different ways of expressing them (e.g. "providing new opportunities for the poor," compared to "providing income maintenance for those with few options") emphasize different aspects of complex and interrelated processes. One of the points that will emerge in the discussion that follows is that different types or categories of MSEs make their principal contribution in terms of different ones of these diverse aspects of the development process.

Heterogeneity and diversity among MSEs

Anyone working in the area of MSEs is conscious of the great heterogeneity of the universe of small producers and traders. A central theme of this study is the search for meaningful patterns of growth for different components of this diverse universe. One of the great and as yet unresolved challenges facing those seeking to understand this field is to find the most meaningful way of classifying these enterprises. Different analysts have focused on a variety of different defining characteristics: differences by size of the enterprise, by location, by gender of the entrepreneur, by sector, or by the degree to which the enterprise obeys the laws and regulations of the country.

Our principal efforts at this categorization are presented in Chapter 7. In that chapter, we suggest an approach based on the past history of the enterprise: its age and past growth experience. In particular, we propose a four-way separation that includes new start-ups; enterprises that have been in existence for some time but have not grown at all in terms of employment since they were established; enterprises that have grown since birth, but only in small amounts; and enterprises that have managed to graduate to the upper end of the small-enterprise spectrum.[6] These different categories of MSEs have different contributions to make to such goals as economic growth and poverty alleviation. Beyond this, our research suggests that different categories of enterprises face different problems and constraints, and can best be helped by different types of interventions.

What this means is that a deeper understanding of patterns of growth among different categories of MSEs, the contributions that these different categories can make to developmental objectives and the problems and constraints faced by each, can enable decision-makers to reach more informed decisions as to appropriate groups on which to concentrate, as well as the kinds of assistance likely to be the most helpful to those particular target groups. It is our hope that the analysis presented here will contribute to that understanding.

The book is organized as follows. Chapter 2 sets the stage by examining various theories of MSE growth, reviewing previous empirical studies and outlining the techniques used in surveys reported on here to gather the primary data on MSEs. The overall growth findings are summarized in Chapter 3, which highlights the turbulent process of MSE creation and closure as well as MSE expansion and contraction. Chapter 4 provides a more disaggregate view of the findings, focusing in more detail on particular locational, sectoral, market linkage, and gender issues concerning MSE growth. The next chapter explores the interrelationships between MSEs and the macroeconomy. Chapter 6 focuses on the problems faced by MSEs, while Chapter 7 sets forth our dynamic categorization of MSEs. The summary and overall implications are reviewed in a concluding chapter.

2 MSE dynamics

Theory and literature review

This chapter reviews the major issues and approaches relating to the analysis of patterns of growth and development among MSEs. Although much has been written in recent years about the nature and structure of such enterprises, the analysis has usually been static in orientation. Firm-level studies of MSE dynamics, both theoretical and empirical, are particularly sparse. Yet the firm is the "client" of assistance programs. This paucity is not limited to developing countries; it is a deficiency that plagues the industrialized countries as well (see e.g. Brock and Evans 1986). The primary aim of this chapter is to correct this imbalance by focusing attention on the central themes that need to be addressed when examining MSEs from a dynamic perspective.

The chapter begins with a review of the relevant theoretical literature and empirical evidence relating to the dynamics of MSEs at the firm level. The key research themes or questions that need to be addressed and analytic approaches that might be used to explore them will then be treated.

Dynamic theories of the firm

The theoretical literature on firm dynamics is quite limited. Some of the more recent theoretical work on industry and firm evolution, however, has generated testable hypotheses about this process. The salient elements of this literature will be briefly highlighted.[1]

The standard, classical theory of the firm sheds little light on the formation, growth or dissolution of individual firms. It is a static equilibrium theory, with no implications for the rate of entry, exit or speed of adjustment. Moreover, it assumes that the supply of entrepreneurs is perfectly elastic, and that no learning occurs within the firm.

Many of the more recent theories of the firm have emphasized the random or stochastic nature of the process of enterprise growth. The primitive versions are based on Gibrat's law, which states that firm growth is independent of firm size (Gibrat 1931). Scherer (1980) provides an illustration of this version, while somewhat more sophisticated variants have been developed by Simon and Bonini (1958) as well as Ijiri and Simon (1977). Such theories, however, accord no independent role for entrepreneurs, assuming rather that they are merely passive actors in a mechanistic game of chance.

Several recent formulations of firm dynamics, such as the models by Lucas (1978) and Kihlstrom and Laffont (1979), have accorded a much more central role for the entrepreneur. A model developed by Jovanovic (1982) synthesizes the key elements of these entrepreneurial models with those of the stochastic models and generates a rich set of testable hypotheses about the life cycle patterns of firm growth. Jovanovic assumes that entrepreneurs have different managerial abilities, yet entrepreneurs are unsure about these abilities when a new business is established. Entrepreneurs gradually "learn" about their abilities by engaging in the rough and tumble business world and observing how well they perform. As they learn more about their own abilities, entrepreneurs change their behavior over time: those who revise their ability estimates upward expand, while those who revise them downward tend to contract or disappear. In general terms, this model indicates that the age and size of the firm play a crucial role in firm dynamics. More specifically, this particular "learning" model predicts that both the firm's failure rates and growth rates will be inversely related to the age and initial size of the individual firm.

Pakes and Ericson (1987) have extended this basic model to allow managerial ability itself to be augmented through human capital formation. Unfortunately, neither the Jovanovic nor the other evolutionary models indicate what the key determinants of this managerial ability might be or how other important variables might affect firm dynamics. Consequently, in generating hypotheses about the key determinants of firm birth, expansion, contraction, and closure, one must ultimately move beyond those suggested by the existing dynamics literature and seek inspiration from empirical sources.

Empirical evidence

The empirical literature sheds additional light on the dynamics of small firms. Insight into this dynamic process can be generated through an examination of the components of the life cycle of these firms. The central elements here are: net firm creation, which itself is made up of firm new starts (births) less firm closures (deaths); and net firm growth, which is composed of expansion of existing firms, less firm contraction. Empirical studies have typically focused on the two net components: firm new starts minus firm closures (net firm creation) and net firm growth. In our discussion, we shall look at each of these components separately.

Firm new starts (births)

In the past, empirical evidence on new start rates of micro and small firms has been limited. Previous estimates suggested annual new start rates for such firms amounting to 8.1 percent in Colombia, 9.6 percent in the United Kingdom, 10.5 percent in the United States, 12.3 percent in Portugal and 12.8 percent in Sierra Leone (Liedholm and Parker 1989; Geroski 1991).[2]

Empirical relationships between new start rates of micro and small firms and other variables have not been systematically examined in any developing country. There is recent evidence from the United States that new start rates are inversely related to firm size; indeed, birth rates of US small firms were found to be three times those of larger firms. Moreover, there is also evidence that new start rates of small firms in the United States have tended to vary directly with the aggregate level of economic activity and have exhibited more year-to-year variations than have the new start rates of their larger scale counterparts (Phillips 1988). Small-firm new start rates also appear to vary by subsector. More specifically, in a recent study of US small firms, Acs and Audretsch (1989) found that the new start rate varied directly with the growth of the subsector and negatively with the four-firm concentration ratio and the level of human capital in the subsector. These empirical relationships found in developed countries may not necessarily hold in developing countries. Microfirm new start rates, for example, might be expected to increase during a decline in the level of aggregate economic activity in many developing countries, if establishing a new micro firm provides the only viable option to individuals who would otherwise be unemployed.

Firm closures

Somewhat more empirical evidence exists on the closure (or death) rates of small firms in developing countries. Firm mortality studies have been undertaken in Sierra Leone, Nigeria, Colombia, the Philippines and India. Nevertheless, even this information is rather scanty. A review of the data generated from these earlier studies suggests that the closure rates of micro firms hover between 9 and 10 percent per year (see Liedholm and Parker 1989).

Several studies have attempted to examine empirically whether systematic patterns exist between closure rates of micro firms and other important variables. Location, sector, size, and age of firm are the variables most often related to firm closures.

The empirical evidence on the relationship between location and closure rates has been rather meager. Data from Sierra Leone (Chuta and Liedholm 1985) indicate that the mortality rates of small firms in rural villages (11.1 percent) are somewhat higher than those for firms located in the largest urban areas (9.5 percent). This relationship was rather weak, however.

Somewhat stronger evidence exists that firm mortality rates vary by sector or subsector. Wide variations in firm disappearance rates by sector, for example, were reported in Frischman's study of microenterprises in Northern Nigeria (Frischman 1988). Unfortunately, significance tests on these relationships were not conducted. In a careful empirical study derived from the Longitudinal Employment Database, which matches information on 300,000 US manufacturing firms from five censuses of manufacturing, Dunne *et al.* (1989) found that industry differences were significant in explaining variations in firm failure rates in the United States.

Most empirical studies have also indicated that mortality rates are inversely related to firm size. Studies from Colombia (Berry and Pinell-Siles 1979) and the Philippines (Anderson 1982), for example, reveal that closure rates decline as one moves to larger size categories of firms.

A similar pattern has been reported in studies conducted in industrialized countries. In the United States, for example, studies by the US Small Business Administration based on data provided by Dun and Bradstreet (Phillips and Kirchhoff 1988) indicate that the death rate of large firms (with 500 or more employees) was one-third that of smaller ones. Dunne *et al.*'s (1989) study of US firms found that "within any age category, failure rates decline with increases in firm size," results that were statistically significant. Similarly, in the United Kingdom, Dunne and Hughes (1994) found a "broad inverse relationship between firm size and the probability of death" from 1980 to 1985. Parallel findings have also been reported for firms in Portugal (Mata and Portugal 1994) and Italy (Arrighetti 1994) during the 1980s. In Germany, however, Wagner (1994) could find no clear relationship between size and firm survival. Yet overall this inverse relationship between failure rates and firm size would appear to be quite strong in both developing and industrialized countries.

One of the relationships found most consistently in empirical studies of firm dynamics is between firm closures and the age of the firm. Virtually all the empirical studies indicate that there is a strong inverse relationship between the age of the firm and the failure rate. Indeed, most disappearances occur during the early years of a firm's existence. Nag's (1980) study of Indian small firms revealed that almost two-thirds of all firm deaths took place during the firm's first four years. In an analysis of age-specific death rates in Sierra Leone, Liedholm (1990) generated estimates of a typical microfirm's "hazard rate," which is the probability that the firm would fail during the following year, given that it has survived until the beginning of that year. At the beginning of the firm's fourth year, for example, the hazard rate was 22 percent, but in the fifth year it declined to 16 percent and in the sixth year it declined to 12 percent.

A similar pattern has been observed in industrialized countries as well. In Dunne *et al*,'s econometric analysis of US manufacturing firms, for example, they found that "the failure rate declines with a firm's age, holding current size fixed" (1989). Parallel findings have been reported for firms in Portugal (Mata and Portugal 1994), Germany (Wagner 1994) and the United Kingdom (Geroski 1991). For small firms, the "hazard rate" in these early years can be quite high. In Portugal, for example, over one-half of the firms with less than ten workers had closed within the first four years (Mata and Portugal 1994). Many firms must confront the grim reality that "life at the bottom of the industry size distribution is, no doubt, nasty, brutish, and short" (Geroksi 1991). These empirical findings that a firm's closure rate is inversely related to both age and size, however, are quite consistent with theoretical predictions derived from the Jovanovic model of firm dynamics.

Given age-specific mortality rates, however, it is possible that firm closure rates might also be affected by the aggregate level of economic activity. Unfortunately, this relationship has not been examined in developing countries. Some insights can be gleaned, however, from a few studies in the United States. In analyzing the relationship between the small-firm failure rates and the aggregate level of economic activity from 1976 to 1986, Phillips and Kirchhoff (1988) found that "death rates exhibited overall stability through time" and were not very sensitive to business cycles; there was a weak direct relationship between closure rates and changes in the level of economic activity. The modest variation that does occur, in fact, might be attributable to variations in firm new start rates in earlier periods. Given typical firm life cycles, for example, a higher than average firm closure rate might be expected three or four years after a surge in birth rates. Support for this notion was provided by Swain and Phillips (1985), who found that firm failure rates in the United States were positively related to firm new start rates in the three previous years, a relationship that held across all firms and in industry-specific analysis. Information of this sort is lacking for micro firms in developing countries.

Net firm growth

The final component to be examined is the net growth (expansion minus contraction) of surviving micro and small firms. The limited evidence that exists on the net growth rates of surviving micro and small firms in developing countries indicates that these rates have been quite high. Indeed, for the three countries where such information exists – Colombia (Cortes *et al.* 1987), India (Little *et al.* 1987), and Northern Nigeria (Chuta 1990) – the annual mean rates of growth of employment are 15.4 percent in Colombia, 16.1 percent in India, and 15.6 percent in Northern Nigeria, figures that cluster remarkably around 15 percent. Although these mean growth rates are quite high, a sizeable group of surviving firms do not grow at all. In Northern Nigeria, for example, 32 percent of the urban micro firms added no workers, while in Sierra Leone (Chuta and Liedholm 1985), 58 percent of small firms in all areas failed to grow.

Empirical regularities between growth rates of firms and other variables have rarely been analyzed in systematic and comprehensive ways, particularly in developing countries. While some attention has been paid to the relationship between growth of the firm and enterprise age and size, other possibly important variables such as sector, location, and gender of the entrepreneur have typically received much less attention.

The relationship between enterprise size and firm growth has been examined in only a few developing countries. Studies by Chuta (1990) in Northern Nigeria found that firms with an initial size of one or two workers expanded at an annual rate of over 30 percent, while firms with an initial size of 10 or more workers declined in size. In Colombia (Cortes *et al.* 1987), the growth rate of employment for metalworking firms was found to be negatively related to initial firm size. A similar pattern was revealed in two South African townships (Liedholm and McPherson 1991). For firms initially with one worker, the annual growth rate was 26.1 percent, while for firms with eight workers or more, the annual growth rate was negative. Such results can only be taken as indicative, however, because these relationships were not rigorously tested.

The relationship between size and growth has been subjected to somewhat more rigorous scrutiny in several studies conducted in industrialized countries. Until recently, most could find little or no correlation between growth rates and size. These studies, however, focused primarily on larger firms only (see e.g. Hart and Prais 1956). More recent analyses in the United States that have included smaller firms have found firm growth to be inversely related to firm size. Evans (1987), using data in the US Establishment Longitudinal Microdata set compiled from 4 million Dun and Bradstreet files and estimating growth rates econometrically using

Heckman's selectivity model, found that firm growth decreases with firm size. This inverse relationship held for 89 percent of the industries he examined in the United States, even after controlling for sample censoring, which arises because of the exit of slow-growing firms from the sample. Dunne *et al.* (1989), using the Longitudinal Employment Database and employing a grouped-data econometric approach to control for sample censoring, also report an inverse relationship between firm growth and firm size. Similar results have been found in the United Kingdom. Following the approach used by Evans (1987), Dunne and Hughes (1994: 137) analyzed data for the United Kingdom and found that: "the results of our analysis shows that both in the late 1970s and early 1980s, the smallest firms were growing faster than the larger ones." These various results are consistent with the predictions from Jovanovic's dynamic model and cast doubt on the validity of Gibrat's law, particularly in developing countries, where small enterprises account for the vast majority of firms in most sectors.

Do the growth rates of micro and small firms vary with the firm's age? The important life cycle aspects of firm growth have rarely been studied in developing countries, yet the age of the firm would appear to be a crucial determinant of firm dynamics. The only studies that have examined this relationship have been conducted in India (Little *et al.* 1987), Colombia (Cortes *et al.* 1987) and Northern Nigeria (Chuta 1990). In all three countries, an inverse relationship was found between the age of the firm and its growth rate. This result held for each of the subsectors examined in these countries. Unfortunately, no statistical tests of significance were conducted in these studies, so the results can only be treated as indicative.

Several studies of small-enterprise dynamics in industrialized countries have rigorously examined the relationship between age and firm growth, including the previously mentioned works of Evans (1987), Dunne *et al.* (1989) and Dunne and Hughes (1994). In the United States, the growth rates of firms were found to decline as the firms aged. Indeed, the negative relationship between growth and age held for 76 percent of the US industrial sectors examined. In the United Kingdom, Dunne and Hughes found that "younger companies, for a given size, grew faster than old companies in the 1980s." The empirical findings as well as those from developing countries are again consistent with deductions from Jovanovic's theory and point to the importance of incorporating life cycle components into any analysis of firm dynamics.

Beyond firm size and age, enterprise growth is affected by an array of demand and supply factors, which are reflected in such measured variables as sector and location. Enterprises in different sectors, for example, face not only varying market demands, but also varying cost structures that could affect growth. Phillips and Kirchhoff (1988) have shown different sectoral patterns of growth for small enterprises in the United States, while Chuta and Liedholm (1985) have found significant sectoral growth variations in Sierra Leone.

Enterprises in different locations also face varying patterns of demand, concentrations of competition, and costs that also influence their growth prospects. Piore and Sabel (1984), among others, for example, have highlighted the advantages that accrue to small firms that group together, particularly in urban areas, and build reliable supplier and buyer relationships within the group. Liedholm and Mead (1987) have presented evidence from five countries indicating that small enterprises operating outside the home and in the larger localities generate more economic profit than others.

There is also evidence of a relationship between entrepreneurial characteristics and firm performance (including growth). Beginning in the 1960s, there have been numerous studies in developing countries seeking to identify empirically the determinants of the evolution of entrepreneurial capacities and their effects on firm performance. These studies, which have been usefully reviewed and summarized by Kilby (1971), Leff (1979), Page (1979) and Anderson (1982), typically conclude that there is no shortage of individuals willing to innovate, bear risks, generate new capital, or expand. Education and experience are frequently found to have a positive influence on business performance, although surprisingly, formal education is sometimes negatively correlated with success, including growth (Chuta and Liedholm 1985). Yet most socio-economic characteristics of entrepreneurs are not generally statistically correlated with performance, suggesting that all segments of the population are potentially capable of contributing to the entrepreneurial pool. These results may be somewhat misleading in a dynamic context, owing to various methodological shortcomings such as the lack of any information on the closed firms and the lack of time series information.

A parallel literature has emerged in recent years that focuses on the gender of the entrepreneur. A number of studies have found that this aspect has an important effect on firm dynamics, particularly on growth and survival chances. Downing (1990) among others argues that female entrepreneurs have goals that are different from those of their male counterparts. Female entrepreneurs, with concerns for income stability and economic security, may be more prone to avoid taking the risks involved with firm expansion and hence may be more likely to diversify instead. The dual domestic and productive responsibilities of female entrepreneurs may also hamper growth and may also mean that business profits may more likely be required to maintain household consumption (Berger 1989).

Moving beyond the gender questions, many of these studies have also found that there are serious and enduring problems with the managerial abilities of the entrepreneurs in many developing countries (Kilby 1988; Anderson 1982). In a dynamic context, the managerial constraint is often said to become particularly acute when a firm attempts to graduate from a microenterprise to a larger size, employing ten or more workers. Indeed, Chuta's (1990) enterprise study of northern Nigeria reported that the managerial abilities of the entrepreneur were the most frequently cited constraint facing firms with six or more workers that are seeking to expand. It is also sometimes argued that policy constraints also may limit this "graduation" process (Liedholm 1990). Empirical evidence on the "graduation" process has been somewhat limited. A study by Liedholm and Parker (1989), based on a re-analysis of firm histories in four African countries (Botswana, Rwanda, Nigeria, and Sierra Leone), two Asian countries (the Philippines and India), and one Latin American country (Colombia), found that relatively few microenterprises graduate or are transformed into modern small or medium enterprises; most remained micro firms. Approached from the other side, the majority of modern small and medium enterprises did not graduate from the micro seedbed, but originated as larger firms in six of the seven countries. The percentage of small and medium firms that were transformed from micro firms was higher in Asia and Latin America than in Africa.

Components of net change in employment

What have been the relative contributions of firm new starts, firm disappearances, and net growth of surviving firms to the overall net change in employment that occurs over time? This can be determined by recognizing that the net change in employment (ΔN) between two points in time would be equal to the employment in new firms (ΔB_N), plus additional employment in expanding firms (ΔG_N), minus the employment loss in firms that contract (ΔC_N), and those that close (die) (ΔD_N). If each of these gross flow components is expressed as a proportion of the employment at the start of the period, the net overall growth rate of employment can be expressed as the sum of the four individual gross component growth rates:

$$\%\Delta N = \%\Delta BN + \%\Delta GN - \%\Delta CN - \%\Delta DN$$

This identity specifies the individual sources of growth or contraction over time that must be separately analyzed, if we are to have a complete picture of the growth process.

Empirical evidence on the relative importance of these four components of net change in employment has only been available for a few developed countries, such as the United States, Canada, and France (Hammermesh 1993). The most striking finding is the sheer magnitude of changes in employment generated by each of the four components. Although the overall net annual change in employment is generally small (less than 1 percent), the four gross flows of employment creation and destruction are individually somewhat larger, ranging from 2.5 to 3.5 percent, for example, in the United States. There is thus a considerable amount of churning among firms. Looking at the relative magnitudes of the individual flows, in the United States, the annual gross changes in employment due to new starts and closures exceed those from the growth and contraction of existing firms. For small firms, in particular, an analysis of data from the United States (Birch 1987) indicates that most of the new jobs resulted from the birth of small firms rather than from the net job expansion of existing firms.

The distinction between net firm creation (new starts less closures) and net firm expansion is important, not only because it sheds light on the vast job churning that takes place among microenterprises, but also because it can provide important clues about the nature of the jobs being created by these firms and forces driving this process. More specifically, employment growth can signal good or bad news. Where the economy is prospering and buoyant aggregate demand results in an expansion of productive enterprises, employment growth can signal prosperity. Yet when the economy is languishing or the population growth rate is high, an increase in employment may simply reflect the bad news that microenterprises are acting as a sponge, soaking up excess workers in marginal activities.[3] In the absence of wage or earnings data, the net firm creation/expansion may provide clues as to the types of jobs being created. If most new start-ups are, in fact, one-person enterprises, these are typically the least economically efficient size category, as indicated in Chapter 1. If these firms subsequently expand, adding even one or two workers, however, there is accumulating evidence that this expansion is associated with significant increases in economic efficiency.[4] To oversimplify a complex set of relationships, jobs arising from net firm expansion are more likely to reflect demand-pull forces while start-up jobs are more likely, on balance, to reflect supply-push forces, as individuals search for activities to sustain themselves.

To this point, the discussion of this chapter has focused primarily on firm growth measured in terms of employment. Less attention has been paid in the literature to an examination of patterns of growth using other measures such as capital stock or output.

Major issues and hypotheses

The major issues and hypotheses to be examined seek to explain and predict the behavior of the key components of the life cycle of individual firms in developing countries. Specifically, these components, which are the dependent variables in the analysis, are the new starts, net growth, and closure (or its inverse, "survival") of individual firms. The central issues that must be addressed involve identifying the key determinants – the independent variables – and how they affect these components of the firm's life cycle.

What are the principal determinants of the new start rate of a micro or small firm in a developing country? The primary explanatory variables for firm new start rates do not arise at the firm level, but rather are external to the firm. Paramount among these external variables are those that operate at the macro and sector level. From the macro level, it would be hypothesized that changes in the aggregate level of economic activity would be expected to influence firm new start rates. Although this relationship is typically found to be positively related in developed countries, it is more likely to be negatively related in developing countries, reflecting the notion that, as the economy worsens, individuals are more likely to be pushed into these activities. It would also be hypothesized that there would be an inverse relationship between firm size and the new start rate, that is birth rates would be expected to decline with increasing size of the enterprise at birth.

The growth and survival (the inverse of firm closure) of firms could be viewed as outcomes of the same economic processes. Consequently, the explanatory variables and the hypotheses formulated for growth and survival can be treated together. Some of these explanatory variables will arise at the firm level, while others could arise either inside the firm (at an individual level) or external to it (at a sectoral or macro level).

Both the growth and survival of micro and small firms would be expected to be influenced by several firm-level variables. Paramount among these would be the age and initial size of the firm. These would be hypothesized to be related to these dependent variables as follows:

1 *Firm age*, reflecting the stage in the life cycle of the enterprise, would be expected to be inversely related to both growth and survival.

2 *Initial size* would also be expected to be inversely related to these variables.

Firm growth and survival would also be expected to be influenced by several factors external to the firm. These include variables such as sector, location, and those at the macroeconomic level.

3 *Sectors* that are growing rapidly and that are not highly concentrated would be more likely to have stronger firm survival and growth rates than those in which the opposite conditions hold.

4 *Location*. It is hypothesized that firm survival and growth would be directly related to locality size. Moreover, firms operating outside the home in visible locations, such as in commercial areas, should have higher growth and survival rates than their counterparts operating from the home.

5 *Macro variables*. Changes in the aggregate level of economic activity would be hypothesized to have a direct effect on small-firm growth and survival in developing countries. In rural areas, changes in the level of agricultural production per capita would be hypothesized to be directly related to rural enterprise survival and growth. The external constraints, including policy, facing these firms are also hypothesized to have an influence on their growth and survival. Moreover, the number of constraints, including the negative effects of policies, are hypothesized to be directly related to the size of the firm; the types of constraints are also expected to vary systematically with the evolution of the enterprise.

Factors internal to the firm, the individual-level variables, would also be hypothesized to affect the survival and growth of a microenterprise. Prominent among these would be the key variables relating to the entrepreneur, such as gender and human capital.

6 *Gender*. Enterprises run by female entrepreneurs are hypothesized to grow less rapidly and to be less likely to survive than those run by their male counterparts.

7 *Human capital*. It is expected that entrepreneurs with higher levels of formal education, technical training, and experience would be more likely to grow and survive than those with lower levels of human capital.

With respect to microenterprise job creation, key issues relate to understanding the patterns of this employment growth. Many of the likely relationships involve the macro-level variables. One hypothesis is that there will be a direct relationship between the changes in the level of economic activity and the relative importance of net firm expansion (along with "graduation") in microenterprise job creation. There is a corresponding hypothesis that there is an inverse relationship between changes in the level of economic activity and the relative importance of new start-up jobs in microenterprise job creation. This reasoning suggests that new start-up jobs are more likely to reflect primarily a press of people seeking a way of sustaining themselves (supply-push), while expansion jobs are more likely to arise as entrepreneurs seek to respond to a growing demand for their products in expanding sectors (demand-pull).

In summary, a wide array of variables, ranging from those emanating from within the firm to those external to the firm, need to be included in any analysis of firm dynamics in developing countries. If the various hypotheses relating these variables are found to be statistically valid, progress will have been made in identifying systematic patterns in the life cycle of these firms.

Analytical approaches and survey methods

New approaches must be used when undertaking studies of firm dynamics in developing countries. This applies to the survey methods needed as well as the analytical procedures chosen.

The information needed for the analysis of firm dynamics in developing countries, for example, is rarely available. Particularly scarce are data on the smallest enterprises, which typically are not captured in government statistics. Even when special surveys of microenterprises are conducted, they tend to focus on the current status of the firm and rarely shed light on its evolution over time.

Moreover, even when dynamic data are collected, they frequently are incorrectly specified. Firm new start rates, for example, are frequently measured in terms of the change in the number of firms in a given period (see Acs and Audretsch 1989). This measure fails to account for firms that disappeared during the period, yielding a measure of net firm creation rather than the desired measure of (gross) new starts. Ideally, the firm new start rate should be calculated by dividing all the new firms appearing in a given time period by the total number of firms in existence at the beginning of the period. One year is the usual time period, so complete counts of the numbers of firms at the beginning and end of the year would be required; the number of firms one year old or less at the end of the year would be considered to be the new starts. Yet even this procedure misses the firms that appeared and then disappeared during the course of the year. This is one manifestation of the sample censoring problem; in this case, the longer the period covered, the greater is the downward bias in estimated new start rates.

Similar difficulties arise in measurements of firm closure rates. Firm closure (death) rates are usually calculated by dividing all firms that can no longer be located at the end of a given time period, typically one year, by the total number of firms in existence at the beginning of that time period. If closures are to be measured, however, then the baseline data at the beginning of the period must be firm specific, a condition not required for birth rate calculations. Furthermore, this procedure once again misses those firms that both are born and die within the period of analysis.

Another important measurement issue centers on the need to generate more precise information on the nature of the closures. In most surveys, a closed firm is one no longer operating in its listed activity at its previous location (Liedholm and Parker 1989). Consequently, a closed firm does not necessarily constitute a business failure; it may simply have changed locations or shifted into a somewhat different line of business. It also may have closed for personal reasons or because a better opportunity arose. Indeed, in some instances, a firm disappearance will be linked to a new firm birth or firm transformation, all elements of the dynamic processes that can only be illuminated by a careful and detailed analysis of firm closures.

What types of survey methods must be employed to generate the needed dynamic information on MSEs in developing countries? Given the weaknesses in the existing data sources and in the conventional survey procedures used to generate them, an array of innovative data collection approaches are needed. These include modified baseline surveys, closed enterprise surveys, tracer surveys, retrospective surveys and panel surveys. The strengths and weaknesses of each of these survey methods will be briefly examined.

Modified MSE baseline surveys

MSE baseline surveys, which involve a door-to-door enumeration of non-agricultural income-earning activities chosen from a stratified random sample of enumeration areas, traditionally have provided a one-shot picture of the numbers, types and location of these enterprises along with the types and numbers of workers. The random selection of locations to be surveyed makes it possible to generalize these findings to generate countrywide estimates. By adding two additional questions relating to the year and number of workers at start-up, however, important dynamic information can also be gleaned that can provide insights on the birth and growth of these enterprises. Details of the conduct of such modified MSE baseline surveys are provided in McPherson and Parker (1993). These surveys have several strengths. They are comprehensive in coverage, generating information on a large number of enterprises, which can serve as the baseline denominator needed for calculating firm new start and closure rates. Moreover, information on the birth year can be used to generate crude estimates of enterprise new start rates as well as, when combined with initial workers at start-up, figures on enterprise employment growth rates since start-up. These baseline surveys, however, cannot provide any insights on the time pattern of this growth and are limited to employment as the growth indicator. Thus, only a narrow picture of the enterprise growth is provided. Moreover, the MSE baseline surveys generate no information on the enterprises that have closed.

Closed enterprise surveys

By extending the MSE baseline survey exercise, it is possible to generate information on those elusive enterprises that have closed. This can be done by undertaking, in the same areas covered by the modified baseline survey, a "closed enterprise" survey. In this case, the door-to-door enumeration would also collect information on businesses previously operated by people in the area but now no longer in operation. Statistics are collected on the size of the business at start-up and at closure, the age of business at closure, and the reasons for this closure. While such surveys can generate comprehensive information on the reasons for and the timing of these closures, they are less useful in determining annual closure rates. This is because, in addition to the recall errors of the respondents (respondents may forget or may choose not to tell about enterprises that have ceased operation), closed enterprises that operated outside the home will tend to be systematically missed in these types of surveys, since the questionnaire asks only about activities that operated at that location.

Tracer surveys

Tracer surveys provide another mechanism for generating information on the dynamics of microenterprises. These surveys seek to determine what has happened over time to a limited number of enterprises (or entrepreneurs) that had been enumerated in some earlier period, typically more than five years previously. Such surveys can generate useful information not only on the time path of enterprise growth, but also on closed enterprise as well. The principal limitations of these surveys are that they usually cover only a few firms initially and even many of these cannot be found, leading to possibly large selectivity biases. Earlier attempts to trace such firms have met with mixed results: 75 percent of the "disappeared" firms were successfully traced in Ecuador (Middleton 1989), but that percentage declined to one-third in Sierra Leone (Chuta and Liedholm 1985) and Nigeria (Frischman 1988).

Retrospective borehole surveys

Another survey approach would be to conduct borehole interviews – retrospective histories – of selected entrepreneurs and their firms, often focusing on particular sectors. These surveys can be undertaken even in those countries where no previous baseline surveys have been conducted. The in-depth, retrospective histories of the entrepreneur and his or her firm can provide important insights into the pattern of change in existing firms and the constraints, both internal and external, that they have faced at different stages in their life cycle. The detailed information can also generate a path analysis of the critical junctures in the development of the firm and entrepreneur. The weaknesses of such surveys are that coverage, as in tracer surveys, is limited, and no information is generated on new start or closure rates.

Panel or prospective surveys

A final survey approach involves conducting longitudinal surveys of existing firms on a repeat basis over a period of time. The traditional method of conducting such panel surveys is to repeatedly sample the same group of respondents quarterly or at least once a year, thereby generating a time series as well as a cross-section data set. Ideally, however, if all the firms in selected areas are included in the panel and the same areas are enumerated each period, all births and closures in these areas will also be detected. Thus, in addition to annual enterprise growth rates, these area-based panel surveys make it possible to generate annual enterprise new start and closure rates. The more frequently these surveys are conducted, the less likely the births and deaths of the short-duration firms will be missed.[5] If flow variables, such as wages and output, are included in the questionnaire, panel surveys can generate annual enterprise growth estimates based on measures other than employment. The disadvantage of panel surveys is they provide information on only a limited period of a firm's life cycle; moreover, they are relatively expensive and resource intensive to administer and analyze.

All five of these survey techniques were used to generate the dynamic information on MSEs that is presented in this book. The surveys and the countries in which they were carried out are summarized in Table 2.1. The most comprehensive data were generated from the six core countries:

Table 2.1 MSE surveys with significant dynamic dimensions: numbers of respondents covered by surveys

Country	*Survey dates*	*Modified baseline survey*	*Closed enterprise survey*	*Panel and repeat baseline surveys*	*Retrospective survey*	*Tracer survey*
(a) Core countries: nationwide surveys with comprehensive data on enterprise dynamics						
Botswana	Feb.–Mar. 1992	1,362	153			
Kenya	Sept.–Oct. 1993	5,353	1,998	May–June 1995	79	
Malawi	June–July 1992	9,672	2,809			
Swaziland	Mar.–Apr. 1991	2,759	650			
Zimbabwe	Aug.–Sept. 1991	5,575	1,101	Sept.–Oct. 1993	40	
Dominican Republic	Mar. 1992	4,568	916	Sept. 1992 Mar. 1993 Mar. 1994		
(b) Other surveys with significant information about enterprise dynamics						
Guinea (one prefecture)	May–June 1993	4,262				
Jamaica	1979–80 to 1994			Apr. 1993–Dec. 1994		142
Lesotho (nationwide survey)	July–Aug. 1990	7,267 (630)				
Niger (two departments)	Oct.–Nov. 1989	18,650				
Nigeria	1961–93					220
South Africa (two townships)	Oct.–Nov. 1990	5,253				

Sources: Botswana: Daniels and Fisseha (1992). Kenya: Parker with Torres (1994); Parker (1994) (for retrospective); Daniels *et al.* (1995) (for repeat baseline). Malawi: Daniels and Ngwira (1993). Swaziland: Fisseha and McPherson (1991). Zimbabwe: McPherson (1991) and (for repeat survey) Daniels (1994); Mead and Kunjeku (1993) (for retrospective survey). Dominican Republic: Cabal (1992, 1993). Guinea: Wierda (1994); this study was sponsored and funded by the Christian Reformed World Relief Committee. Jamaica: Fisseha (1994) (for tracer); Gustafson and Liedholm (1995) (for panel). Lesotho: Fisseha (1991). Niger: Fisseha (1990). Nigeria: Kilby (1994). South Africa: Liedholm and McPherson (1991).

Notes: For all surveys in part (a) of the table, the baseline questionnaire included information about starting year and employment at start-up. This was also true for the surveys in the Dominican Republic, Guinea, and South Africa. The surveys in Guinea, Niger, and South Africa covered only selected regions or locations, while the surveys in the Dominican Republic and Lesotho were nationwide. In Lesotho, dynamic questions were asked only in the supplementary questionnaire (numbers shown in parentheses). The retrospective investigation in Kenya was limited to woodworking and footwear enterprises; that in Zimbabwe focused on leather and footwear, garments, and metal products.

Botswana, Kenya, Malawi, Swaziland, Zimbabwe, and the Dominican Republic. Somewhat less comprehensive data were collected from Guinea, Jamaica, Lesotho, Niger, Nigeria, and South Africa.

The baseline surveys have reached a large number of small enterprises in these twelve countries. In the core countries, the first six countries listed in Table 2.1, the baseline questionnaire was administered to 28,000 respondents. Much of our subsequent analysis focuses on those six, which provide us with the richest body of data about small-enterprise dynamics. Other countries on the supplementary list include three where the modified baseline survey was administered, but only in certain localities (Guinea, South Africa) or to a smaller sample of respondents nationwide (Lesotho), and three others where other types of dynamic information are available (Niger, Nigeria, and Jamaica). Adding all these countries with some type of dynamic survey information, we reach a total of nearly 65,000 respondents in twelve countries.

It is obvious that the achievement of such wide coverage has involved important trade-offs, severely limiting the type of information that it was possible to collect. There are a great many questions about which all of us would like to know more, but the collection of such information was seen as not feasible in fast-moving questionnaires using enumerators who often had only limited understanding of the topics being examined.

The information generated by these various surveys has been analyzed in a variety of ways to illuminate firm-level dynamics in developing countries. These approaches can range in complexity from simple tabular presentations of the key relationships to more sophisticated statistical and econometric analyses. The data analysis approaches are discussed, where relevant, in the chapters that follow.

Summary

Most economic theory of the firm focuses on equilibrium conditions; as such, it is of little help in explaining patterns of change at the level of the individual firm. A review of existing empirical literature suggests several possible factors that appear to influence patterns of enterprise dynamics. Among these, the most important are: enterprise age and size, sector and location; characteristics of the entrepreneur, including the gender and the level of human capital of the owner; and macro factors, relating to the broader context in which the enterprise operates. Each of these might be hypothesized to influence patterns of enterprise births, closures and growth.

3 New starts, closures, and expansion of MSEs

Overview

MSEs are constantly evolving. Most of these changes are missed, however, if one focuses only on the aggregate changes in the level of MSE activity over time. It is only when the individual components of these changes are scrutinized that the magnitude of this churning becomes apparent. Not only are new firms being created (new starts, or enterprise births) while others are closing, but existing (surviving) firms are expanding and contracting. These components of change are sometimes summarized in two concepts: net firm creation, which is new starts minus closures; and net firm expansion, which is firm expansion less firm contraction. Since the individual components move in opposite directions, however, these net measures of change mask the magnitude of the churning that is taking place among MSEs.

In this chapter, the key survey findings on these individual components of change are examined. Specifically, the empirical evidence on new starts, closures, and existing firm growth (net firm expansion) will be scrutinized. Such an individual focus is important because each of these is subject to different forces, with different possible intervention implications.

New MSE starts

Empirical evidence on new business starts (firm creation) in developing countries has been virtually non-existent until recently. New findings from surveys in the six core countries, summarized in Table 3.1, reveal that the rate of new MSE starts is very high. The annual rate of MSE new starts in these countries averages over 20 percent, ranging in a narrow band from 19.3 percent in Zimbabwe to 25.2 percent in Botswana. Although the approaches used to collect the data mean that they are still not as accurate as we would wish, they are broadly indicative and, given the techniques used, provide lower-bound estimates of the orders of magnitude involved.[1] These surprising high figures are substantially above the 10 percent rate typically reported for small enterprises in industrialized countries.

What is the relationship between the new starts and enterprise size? An examination of Table 3.1 reveals that, at least for Africa, there is a strong inverse relationship between the two. The average annual new start rate for the ubiquitous one-person firm, for example, is almost 30 percent, while the corresponding rate for firms over ten workers is typically less than 10 percent. Most of the churning in these countries is taking place among the smallest firms.

It is thus not surprising that the vast majority of the new firms being created are one-person establishments. In the six core survey countries, in fact, these self-employed firms comprise almost 80 percent of the new starts (see Table 3.2).

Not much is known about the central forces driving the MSE new start rates. A recent study by Daniels (1995) looking at MSEs in Zimbabwe indicates that the determinants of new starts differ between high- and low-profit activities. For high-return activities, initial capital requirements, experience of the entrepreneur, and level of regulation are all inversely related to the new start rate. For low-return activities, the rate of new starts is related (inversely) only to the aggregate level of economic activity; for these firms, the lower the level of aggregate economic activity, the higher the rate of new starts, reflecting the importance of the push factor in firm creation.

An important implication of these findings is that there is no overall

Table 3.1 Annual MSE new starts rate – by initial size, Africa and Latin America

Country	*Year*	*Enterprise size (number of workers)* 1	2–9	10+	*Overall average*
Botswana	91	32.9%	11.5%	4.2%	25.2%
Kenya	92	33.7%	10.3%	1.6%	21.2%
Malawi	91	26.9%	14.1%	13.1%	21.7%
Swaziland	90	26.3%	10.8%	2.4%	21.7%
Zimbabwe	90	22.8%	10.6%	18.7%	19.3%
Dominican Republic	93	n.a.	n.a.	n.a.	20.6%
Average		28.5%	11.5%	8.0%	21.6%

Source: Computed from individual country survey data. Averages are unweighted across the six countries.

Table 3.2 Percentages of new starts – by initial size

Country	*Enterprise size (number of workers)*			
	1	*2–9*	*10+*	*All sizes*
Botswana	74.9%	24.2%	0.4%	100%
Kenya	71.2%	28.1%	0.7%	100%
Malawi	76.1%	23.0%	0.9%	100%
Swaziland	85.6%	14.1%	0.3%	100%
Zimbabwe	83.2%	15.8%	1.0%	100%
Average	78.2%	21.1%	0.7%	100%

Source: Computed from individual country survey data.

scarcity of entrepreneurs in the sense of individuals willing to incur the risk of establishing a new venture. Most of these new starts are one-person firms, which are typically the least efficient and remunerative of the MSEs; they tend to enter in greater numbers when the overall economy is languishing. Given these findings, direct programmatic support of new starts should be undertaken only after careful consideration of other available options.

MSE closures

Survey results indicate that MSE closure rates are also quite high. The annual rate of closures of MSEs in the Dominican Republic, the country with the most accurate annual figures, exceeded 20 percent in the early 1990s.[2] The Dominican Republic findings, which are probably typical, highlight the extreme volatility of MSE activity, where simultaneously one large segment is starting just as another large segment of MSEs is closing.

Why do these MSEs close? The survey results make clear that only a portion, frequently a minority, of the closures can be attributed to the traditional "business failure," where the firm is not financially or economically viable. As a glance at Table 3.3 reveals, only about one-half of the MSE closures in the six core countries were due to "bad business conditions." Lack of demand and shortage of working capital were the two most frequently mentioned underlying external causes of these traditional "business failures."[3] For the others, approximately one-quarter of the MSEs closed for personal reasons of the entrepreneur, such as illness or retirement. Another 10 percent shut down because the entrepreneur was able to move on to better options, such as newly emerging, more profitable entrepreneurial opportunities. Another 5 percent of the enterprises were forcibly closed by the government, perhaps because they were operating in an illegal location or were not meeting other government requirements or regulations.

What are the characteristics of the closed firms? Among the variables likely to be systematically related to firm closures are the enterprise age, sector, location, growth, and size of the enterprise, along with the gender and ethnic origin of the entrepreneur. Governmental policy may also enter as an important determinant of enterprise closures. The evidence generated by the country closed enterprise surveys plus recent statistical analyses of firm closures in Swaziland and Zimbabwe by McPherson (1992) and in the Dominican Republic by Cabal (1995) provide new insights into this phenomenon.

One of the strongest and most consistent empirical relationships is that between firm closure and the age of the firm. Table 3.4 reveals a strong inverse relationship between the age of the firm and the closure rates in Southern Africa. Most closures occur in the early years of the firm's existence. In four of the five survey countries, for example, over 50 percent of the closures had taken place by the end of the firm's third year. Malawi was the lone exception in this regard, with only one-third of the firms closing by that time. This pattern of early closure is similar to that observed in India and the United States. In Kenya and Zimbabwe, the closures peak between the first and second years, while in Swaziland and Botswana they peak during the first year.[4]

What are the characteristics of the MSEs that close and how, if at all, do these differ from the characteristics of the survivors? The results of systematic analyses of closure patterns of MSEs in Swaziland, Zimbabwe (McPherson 1992), and the Dominican Republic (Cabal 1995) make it possible to paint an initial portrait of the type of enterprise that is most

Table 3.3 Reasons for closure of MSEs (in percent of enterprises)

Reason	*Botswana*	*Kenya*	*Malawi*	*Swaziland*	*Zimbabwe*	*Dominican Republic*	*Average*
Business conditions bad	43	36	54	56	47	53	47
Better options	21	9	8	6	7	4	10
Personal reasons	28	31	21	22	28	27	26
Government action/ natural disaster	2	6	3	4	6	2	4
Other	15	18	14	12	12	14	14
Total	100	100	100	100	100	100	100

Source: Survey data.
Note: Average is unweighted.

Table 3.4 Age distribution of closed enterprises (%)

Age at closure (years)	*Botswana*	*Kenya*	*Swaziland*	*Zimbabwe*	*Overall average*
<1	16	17	21	13	15
1	11	22	16	18	15
2	10	16	12	17	13
3	11	11	7	10	9
4	6	7	8	9	8
5	6	5	4	6	6
6	4	3	4	5	4
7	7	2	3	4	4
>7	29	17	25	18	26

Source: Survey data.

likely to survive. These studies have made use of a technique called "hazard analysis" to ascertain the key factors that determine the closure and survival patterns of such enterprises. The dependent variable in this analysis is the "hazard rate," which is the probability that a firm will close during the given year. The independent variables used to explain this rate are such variables as the age, sector, and location of the firm. Econometric techniques are used to estimate the relationships.[5] The findings of these studies are summarized in Table 3.5.

What are the salient characteristics of MSEs that are most likely to survive? In addition to age, the past growth patterns, initial size, sector, location, and gender of the owner might be expected to play a role.

An important finding from these studies is the recognition that growing MSEs were more likely to survive than those that remained the same size. More specifically, the results from Zimbabwe and Swaziland indicate that for every 1 percent increase in employment, the MSE reduced its likelihood of closing during the year by approximately 5 percent (McPherson 1992). Such findings are consistent with the notion that expanding MSEs have become more efficient – or, perhaps, were more efficient to start with – and are thus more able to survive.

One of the most surprising results, however, was the discovery that the expected direct relationship between the MSE's initial size and its survival chances was not supported by the data. In fact, a result opposite from that posited by theory was obtained. Firms that started the smallest, other factors being held constant, were more likely to survive than their counterparts that started larger.[6] This finding indicates that smallness, by itself, is no impediment to survival.

The survival rates of MSEs also varied significantly by sector. In all three countries, retail trading MSEs faced the highest closure risks; these

Table 3.5 Key determinants of MSE survival and growth

	Survival likelihood (higher if MSE)	*Growth likelihood (higher if MSE)*
Age	Older	Younger
Past growth	Grown in past	–
Initial size	Smaller*	Smaller*
Sector	Not in trading	In particular sectors that vary by country
Location	Urban, not in home	Urban, not in home
Gender	Male owned	Male owned

Sources: Derived from findings of McPherson (1992), for Swaziland and Zimbabwe, and Cabal (1995) for the Dominican Republic.
*Not significant in the Dominican Republic.

firms were almost 30 percent more likely to close during the year, for example, than their woodworking counterparts. Real estate, wood processing, wholesale traders, and non-metallic metal enterprises were the least likely to close, while those engaged in trading, transport, and chemical MSEs were the most likely to do so, in the two African countries covered by this analysis.[7]

Another striking and powerful finding is that location appears to play a central role in determining MSE survival. Urban MSEs in the two African countries had an almost 25 percent greater chance of surviving the year, holding all other factors constant, than their counterparts in rural areas.[8] In addition, MSEs located in commercial districts were more likely to survive than those that operated out of the home. Proximity to growing markets would thus seem to contribute in an important way to enterprise survival.

MSE survival rates also varied significantly by the gender of the entrepreneur. More specifically, female-headed MSEs were less likely to survive than their male-headed counterparts, all other factors constant. This analysis is based on an examination of the survival and closing of MSEs due to all factors. A relatively high percentage of the closings of female-headed MSEs in these countries, however, was due to personal and other non-business reasons. When only closings due to pure business failures were analyzed separately, the gender of the entrepreneur was no longer a significant determinant. Thus, in terms of closings due to business failures only, female-headed and male-headed MSEs were equally likely to survive.

Finally, at a more macro level, there is limited and mixed evidence from Zimbabwe and the Dominican Republic that changes in the overall level of economic activity also affect MSE closure rates. For low-return activities in Zimbabwe, Daniels (1995) found closure rates to be negatively related to the country's growth rate;[9] thus, as the overall level of economic activity increases, the likelihood that MSEs would survive the year increases as well. Yet findings from a similar study of MSEs in the Dominican Republic (Cabal 1995) suggest the opposite relationship holds: when aggregate growth rates increase, MSE survival rates decline. These results will be explored in more detail in Chapter 5.

These closure findings provide important insights into the relative riskiness of various client groups that are included in the portfolio of MSE existing or planned projects and programs. Those projects that wish to minimize the riskiness of their client portfolios might want to focus their attention on MSEs that have grown, that have existed longer than three years, and that operate in commercial districts in urban areas, in sectors other than trading. Alternatively, for programs focusing on the more risky MSEs, the findings provide a basis for incorporating these risk factors into their performance evaluations.

Net MSE expansion

To these changes resulting from the establishment of new firms and the closure of others must be added the growth from the net expansion of existing enterprises over time. The net expansion depicts the expansion less the contraction of those MSEs that survive; it summarizes two opposing dynamic forces at work.

The change in the number of workers since start-up is the indicator typically used to measure the magnitude of the net expansion of MSEs and the one used in the surveys reported in this study. This measure tends to be favored because it is most easily and accurately remembered by the entrepreneur and because it does not need to be deflated.

What biases might arise from the use of employment as a measure of expansion rather than alternative indicators such as changes in sales, output, or assets? Although data on these other indicators are limited, some recent surveys have begun to illuminate this issue. Parker's (1994) analysis of the growth in Kenyan MSEs, for example, found that net increases in real sales were almost double the growth in employment. A similar pattern was found in the Jamaican Quarterly Panel Survey of MSEs (Gustafson and Liedholm 1995), where the change in real sales was twice the change in employment. Such findings highlight the lumpy nature of employment, which appears to increase with a lag after a sizeable growth in real sales, suggesting that the employment growth measures provide a lower-bound, relatively conservative, estimate of net firm expansion.

One of the most striking findings to emerge from the various surveys is the high average growth rates exhibited by existing (surviving) MSEs. Table 3.6 indicates that the average annual compound employment growth rate since start-up was 8.7 percent per year in the eight countries with relevant data.[10] The country variations around this average are large, however, ranging from 2.4 percent in Lesotho to 24.0 percent in Kenya.

These high average growth rates are all the more impressive when it is recognized that, except for Botswana and Lesotho, they are at least double the overall growth in GDP in these countries during the 1980s. Moreover, in absolute terms, the annual number of new jobs created per enterprise is impressive (see Table 3.6, third column).

When MSE employment growth of existing firms is examined year to year rather than from start-up, there is also evidence of net MSE contraction during certain periods. In Jamaica, for example, employment in existing MSEs declined almost 10 percent from 1993 to 1994 (Gustafson and

Table 3.6 Annual employment growth of existing MSEs: alternative measures (annual change since start-up)

Country	*Annual growth rate: average growth measure[a] (%)*	*Annual growth rate: compound growth measure[b] (%)*	*Annual change in number of jobs per firm (number)[c]*
Botswana	8.4	6.3	0.119
Kenya	29.0	24.0	0.297
Lesotho	5.9	2.4	0.094
Malawi	10.5	9.0	0.112
Swaziland	6.6	4.1	0.061
Zimbabwe	7.4	5.6	0.084
Southern/Eastern Africa – average	11.3	8.6	0.128
Niger	8.5	5.7	0.101
Dominican Republic	15.1	12.6	0.157
World – average	11.4	8.7	0.128

Sources: Swaziland, Fisseha and McPherson (1991); Lesotho, Fisseha (1991); Zimbabwe, McPherson (1991); Kenya, Parker with Torres (1994); Dominican Republic, Cabal (1992); Botswana, calculated from data generated by Daniels and Fisseha (1992); Niger, calculated from data generated by Joumard *et al.* (1992); Malawi, calculated from data generated by Daniels and Ngwira (1993).

Notes:

[a] Average annual growth rate in terms of employment is calculated as: (Current Employment – Initial Employment/Initial Employment)/ Firm Age.

[b] Annual compound growth in employment is calculated as: $[(\text{Current Employment}/\text{Initial Employment})^{(1/\text{Firm Age})}] - 1$.

[c] Average annual growth in jobs since start-up is calculated as: (Current Employment – Initial Employment)/Firm Age.

Liedholm 1995), while in the Dominican Republic over the same period, the decline was 3.2 percent (Cabal 1995). The role of the overall economy in explaining these short-run variations will be examined in Chapter 5.

These generally rapid average growth rates are all the more impressive when it is recognized that the majority of MSEs in survey countries did not grow at all since start-up. As indicated in Table 3.7, less than 30 percent of the MSEs had added any workers at all since their start; approximately two-thirds remained the same size.[11] MSE employment expansion was the exception rather than the rule, and the overall net expansion was thus being propelled by a minority of the enterprises. Nor was it true that it was only the young firms that had not grown. In Swaziland, for example, 46 percent of the firms that remained the same size had been in operation for five years or more. The longer the firm survives, however, the less likely it is that it will remain the same size. In Swaziland, once again, 85 percent of one-year-old firms had not grown, while only 62 percent of the firms more than four years old had not expanded (Fisseha and McPherson 1991).

Another significant finding is that most of the growing MSEs added only a few workers. Of those MSEs that had grown, over 90 percent added less than four workers. About 5 percent of the expanding MSEs "graduated" from the microenterprise seedbed and ended up with more than ten workers. Thus, the largest share of the employment expansion was due to a relatively small share of all MSEs that grew; but of those that grew, most expanded by adding only a few workers.

When an existing MSE expands by adding even one or two workers, it is quite likely that this will be associated with a significant increase in its economic efficiency as well as in its net income. Most new MSE start-ups are one-person enterprises, which is also the least efficient size category (see discussion in Chapter 1). If some of these MSEs subsequently expand, adding even one more worker, they will be moving into a size category where their economic efficiency as well as their net income are likely to be significantly higher.[12] Moreover, the jobs created should be more enduring and should generate higher returns.

What are the characteristics of those enterprises that are most likely to expand and how, if at all, do they differ from those that do not grow? Such information is important given the economic significance of MSE expansion. The results of a systematic analysis of the determinants of growth in the six core countries along with Lesotho make it possible to provide a profile of the types of MSE most likely to expand. Following McPherson (1995), statistical techniques were used to test whether or not the key independent variables discussed in Chapter 2, such as age, initial size, sector, location, country, gender of entrepreneur, and human capital, were

Table 3.7 Composition of employment change in MSEs (percentage of firms by category)

Country	*No change*	*Expanded*	*Contracted*
Botswana	75.7	19.0	5.3
Kenya	59.6	37.6	2.8
Lesotho	73.6	18.2	8.2
Malawi	75.0	23.0	2.0
South Africa	49.4	48.3	2.3
Swaziland	68.9	28.3	2.3
Zimbabwe	77.0	19.3	3.7
Southern/Eastern Africa	68.5	27.7	3.8
Niger	44.8	37.4	17.8
Sierra Leone	58.0	39.0	3.0
Dominican Republic	67.3	29.1	3.6
Average – overall	65.0	29.9	5.1

Sources: Sierra Leone, Chuta and Liedholm (1985). For other countries, same as Table 3.6.

significantly related to the dependent variable, enterprise growth, since start-up.[13] The overall findings, which are summarized in Table 3.5, will now be examined.

The analysis revealed, consistent with theory, that there was an inverse relationship between the age of the MSE and expansion. Thus, it was the younger MSEs that were most likely to generate more expansion jobs. Similar results were reported in the Dominican Republic (Cabal 1995) and Kenya (Parker 1994). Examining the growth and age performance of individual MSEs over time, however, Parker (1994) found that the inverse age and growth relationship held only for MSEs that started with one worker or with more educated entrepreneurs. Much of the expansion occurred in the first two years in the life of the enterprise. After the eighth year, a common pattern of downsizing took place, however, among MSEs of all types and sizes.

Another important finding was the significant inverse relationship between initial size and growth of the MSE. This result was consistent with the hypothesized relationship discussed in Chapter 2. The smaller MSEs at start-up thus added more expansion jobs per firm than did their larger-scale counterparts, a powerful finding for those concerned with employment creation. Parallel findings have been reported elsewhere in Africa (Parker 1994; McPherson 1995), although a direct relationship between initial size and growth was found in the Dominican Republic (Cabal 1995).[14]

The sector in which an MSE operates was also found to be an important determinant of growth. At the most aggregate sectoral level, MSEs in manufacturing and services were more likely to expand than those in trading. At a more disaggregated level, however, the specific sectors that were likely to generate more MSE expansion varied from country to country. In Swaziland, for example, MSEs in non-metallic minerals expanded substantially less than retail trading, while in Kenya all sectors, including non-metallic minerals, expanded more rapidly than retail trading. What these findings suggest is that sectoral differences are significant at the country level in explaining MSE expansion, reflecting perhaps each country's comparative advantage – its unique fingerprint. At the same time, no universal sectoral growth patterns emerged. These sectoral issues are examined in more detail in the next chapter.

Location was another factor identified by the analysis as a determinant of MSE expansion. MSEs located in urban areas were more likely to grow than their rural-based counterparts. Moreover, MSEs operating in commercial districts or even alongside the road showed a markedly stronger tendency to expand than did those operating from the home. Other studies have yielded similar results, but with a few local variations. McPherson (1995) found, for example, that MSEs in Southern Africa operating in even traditional markets were more likely to expand than home-based firms, while Cabal (1995) found that size of locality had no effect on the likelihood of expansion in the Dominican Republic.

The analysis also revealed that male-headed MSEs were more likely to expand than female-headed ones, even when controlling for such variables as sector and location. Although similar results have been reported by McPherson (1995) and Parker (1994), it is noteworthy that ownership gender proved not to be statistically significant in the Dominican Republic (Cabal 1995). These findings will be explored in greater depth in the following chapter.

Although "human capital" could not be included in the formal statistical analysis owing to data limitations, related studies provide evidence that it does significantly affect MSE expansion. McPherson (1992) reported that entrepreneurs in Southern Africa with vocational training expanded their MSEs 9 percent faster than those without such training. For Kenya, Parker (1994) found that entrepreneurs who had at least seven years' experience were likely to expand their business more rapidly than those without such experience. It was also found that entrepreneurs who had completed secondary school were more likely to expand in Kenya (Parker 1994), Zimbabwe (McPherson 1992), and the Dominican Republic (Cabal 1995).[15] Completion of primary school by the entrepreneur, however, was found to have no significant effect on MSE expansion in any of these countries.

Finally, at the more macro level, there is evidence of a direct relationship between the level of economic activity and MSE expansion. The higher the level of overall economic activity, the greater the amount of MSE expansion. This relationship will be examined in more detail in Chapter 5.

Facilitating an expansion of existing MSEs can contribute to increased economic efficiency and higher returns to the enterprise while generating jobs that are more likely to endure. The growth analysis, by providing statistical support for the previously outlined hypotheses on the determinants of growth, yields important clues as to the forces leading to enterprise expansion. Assistance programs need to work with these forces, taking advantage of them wherever possible. This might mean reinforcing and strengthening the positive attributes of any particular client group. It might mean linking rural firms with more dynamic urban markets, or seeking to expand access to more effective educational programs. Carefully crafted programs designed to facilitate a switch to expanding product lines might contribute in important ways to this process. The implications of these findings for programs and projects are explored in more detail in Chapter 7.

Summary

There are three principal dimensions of change among MSEs: births, closures, and growth. Data on new starts indicate enterprise birth rates averaging about 20 percent per year. These birth rates are even higher for the very small enterprises, and for enterprises owned by women. These high rates suggest that there is no overall scarcity of entrepreneurs ready to launch new ventures.

Although less information is available, it appears that closure rates for MSEs are also high. Estimates from the Dominican Republic suggest rates of over 20 percent per year. Closure rates are highest in the early years of an enterprise's existence, with more than half of reported closures taking place within the first three years. Many closures do not result from a failure of the business but rather personal factors in the owner's life (e.g. illness, old age) or else a decision to move on to other, preferable, opportunities. Enterprises are more likely to survive if they are older, if they started smaller, if they are located in close proximity to the market, and if they are owned by males. Enterprises that had grown in the past were more likely to survive, as were those in some specific sectors of the economy.

While only a minority of all enterprises had grown in terms of employment since their start, overall growth rates are high, averaging

8–11 percent per year. Growth rates were higher in the early years of the enterprise's life, in those that started smaller, and in those located close to more dynamic markets. Average growth rates varied significantly by sector, although the patterns of growth varied from country to country, with no particular sectors showing consistently high growth rates across all countries.

4 MSE growth by location, sector, linkages, and gender

The discussion of preceding chapters has made clear that patterns of MSE growth vary by location, by sector, by the nature of the market linkages joining the different participants in the system, and by gender of the owner of the enterprise. In this chapter, each of these four dimensions will be examined in more detail to ascertain their influence on patterns of growth of small enterprises.

Growth patterns by location

The locational variations, particularly the differences between rural and urban MSEs, will be examined first. Rural enterprise growth patterns and the role of agriculture in this process will receive particular scrutiny.

A brief review of the structural profile findings reminds us why a rural focus is important. Over 70 percent of the enterprises and employment in the survey countries in Africa are located outside of urban areas. MSE densities (number of MSEs, or numbers of people working in MSEs, per 1,000 people in the population) are sometimes higher and sometimes lower as one moves from urban to more rural localities. Perhaps surprisingly, manufacturing generally constitutes a larger share of enterprises in rural than in urban areas.

How do the dynamic patterns of growth of rural enterprises differ from those of their urban counterparts? Locational differences in new enterprise starts (births) and closures will be examined first, followed by a review of differences in growth through net firm expansions.

The data on MSE new start rates disaggregated by locality size are summarized in Table 4.1. They present a somewhat mixed picture. Rural enterprise new start rates are at least 4 percentage points higher than those in urban areas in Botswana and are somewhat higher in Swaziland. A similar locational pattern of new starts has also been reported for the Dominican Republic, where the new start rate in rural areas (28.8

percent) exceeded that in urban areas (24.5 percent) during the 1992–3 period (Cabal 1993). In two other African countries, however, the opposite pattern is found, with urban new start rates somewhat higher than their rural counterparts.[1] These differences may be explained by such factors as the performance of the agricultural sector as well as the level and rate of growth of overall economic activity in these countries.

Figures on enterprise closure rates disaggregated by size of locality are particularly scarce. In the Dominican Republic, the only country for which the requisite figures exist, the annual enterprise closure (death) rate in rural areas (33.8 percent) was substantially higher than that in urban areas (24.5 percent) in 1992–3 (Cabal 1993). In that country, new start and closure rates followed the same locational pattern (i.e. both are higher in rural areas). The "hazard analysis," which was described earlier and was designed to provide a picture of the characteristics of enterprises that are most likely to close, also indicated that, in the five core African countries, rural enterprises were more likely to close than their counterparts located in urban areas (Liedholm *et al.* 1994). The overall pattern of growth of existing enterprises also varies significantly by location. As indicated in Table 4.2, in all countries except Kenya, enterprises located in urban areas grew significantly more rapidly than those in rural areas. Indeed, the world-wide average growth rate for urban enterprises was over 4 percentage points higher than that for rural enterprises; in several countries the urban rate was more than double the rural rate.

One of the reasons for the relatively slower rural growth rates is that typically fewer rural enterprises were expanding. The percentage of MSEs that grew was lower in rural than in urban areas in four of the five survey countries (Liedholm and Mead 1994). The highest percentage of rural

Table 4.1 Annual birth rates by size of locality

Country	*Annual birth rate (percent per year)*				
	Year	*Urban*	*Rural town*	*Rural EA*	*Overall*
Botswana	91	22.7	24.2	27.1	25.3
Kenya	92	22.4	20.4	21.2	21.2
Malawi	91	23.4	20.8	21.5	21.7
Swaziland	90	19.5	20.5	22.3	21.7
Zimbabwe	90	20.6	18.7	18.6	19.3
Average		21.7	20.8	22.1	21.8

Source: Computed from individual country survey data.

Notes: Rural town refers to rural townships, which are locations with from 2,000 to 20,000 inhabitants; rural EA refers to rural enumeration areas, which are locations with fewer than 2,000 inhabitants.

Table 4.2 Annual employment growth rate of existing MSEs[a] – "average" growth rate measure

	Growth rate (%)		
Country	*Urban*	*Rural*[b]	*Entire country*
Botswana	11.6	7.0	8.4
Kenya	25.0	30.0	29.0
Lesotho	12.2	4.3	5.9
Malawi	15.7	9.9	10.5
South Africa	23.9	–	–
Swaziland	12.3	5.6	6.6
Zimbabwe	9.0	6.7	7.4
Southern/Eastern Africa	15.7	10.6	11.3
Nigeria[c]	15.6	–	–
Ghana[c]	11.9	–	–
Niger	8.5	8.4	8.5
Colombia[d]	15.4	–	–
Dominican Republic	16.4	13.1	15.1
India[c]	16.1	–	–
World-wide	14.9	10.6	11.4

Sources: South Africa, Liedholm and McPherson (1991); Swaziland, Fisseha and McPherson (1991); Lesotho, Fisseha (1991); Zimbabwe, McPherson (1991); Kenya, Parker and Aleke Dondo (1991); Nigeria, Chuta (1990); Ghana, Steel and Webster (1990); Colombia, Cortes *et al.* (1987); Dominican Republic, Cabal (1992); India, Little *et al.* (1987); Botswana, calculated from data generated by Daniels and Fisseha (1992); Niger, Joumard *et al.* (1992); Malawi, calculated from data generated by Daniels and Ngwira (1993).

Notes:

[a] Average annual growth rate in terms of employment and is defined as follows: $[(A - B)/B]/C$ where: A = number of workers now: B = number of workers when enterprise started; and C = number of years firm has been in existence. [b] Rural includes rural areas (enumeration areas) plus secondary towns. [c] Manufacturing enterprises only. [d] Metal firms only.

growers was found in Kenya, where over one-third of the MSEs had expanded. Among the enterprises that did expand, it is noteworthy that in two countries, Kenya and Botswana, the percentage of such enterprises that "graduated" (i.e. started out with less than five workers but subsequently grew to more than ten workers) was higher in rural than in urban areas.

To what degree has agriculture played a role in explaining the performance of rural enterprises in the countries surveyed? Although a paucity of both time series and cross-section data preclude rigorous statistical analysis, some indicative insights may be gleaned.

In a study examining the determinants of rural MSE growth in the five core African studies, Liedholm *et al.* (1994) found that the overall performance of rural enterprises stood out in two countries, Botswana and Kenya. Not only were the existing rural firm growth rates in these two countries among the highest (see Table 4.2), but the percentage of the overall growth coming from firm expansion rather than from new starts was significantly higher in these two countries.

What might account for this differential country performance? The overall macroeconomic conditions, both in terms of level and growth of per capita income during the decade of the 1980s, might explain the relatively successful rural enterprise performance in Botswana, whose per capita income level ($2,790 in 1992) and growth rate of GNP per capita (6.1 percent per year from 1980 to 1992) were exceptional within Africa. Yet they do not explain what happened in Kenya, whose overall macro indicators (1992 GNP per capita of $310 and annual GNP per capita growth of +2 percent) more closely resembled those of Malawi (1992 GNP per capita of $210 and annual GNP per capita growth of −0.1 percent).

The overall performance of the agricultural sectors of these economies during this period, however, would be expected to be a crucial macro determinant of rural enterprise performance. This relationship has long been reflected in the agricultural growth linkage formulations of Mellor (1976), Johnston and Kilby (1975), and others, where rural enterprise growth is a demand-driven spinoff of agricultural growth. Consumption as well as backward and forward production linkages play key roles in these models.

An examination of the published figures (World Bank 1993) on the annual growth of food production per capita from 1980 until 1991 reveals that Kenya was the only country among the five to experience positive growth. Food production per capita increased at an annual rate of 0.5 percent and the demand-driven spinoff from it no doubt served to propel Kenya's rural enterprise sector. During the same period, food production per capita was negative in Malawi (−2.7 percent), Swaziland (−0.9 percent), Zimbabwe (−1.0 percent), and even Botswana (−3.7 percent). Agriculture was clearly not central in explaining rural enterprise performance in Botswana, since agriculture accounted for less than 5 percent of GNP in that country and other sources of demand predominated. Its role in the other countries, however, was clearly important. This appears to be particularly true in understanding the desultory performance of rural enterprises in Swaziland; not only were the percentage of small starters that had grown or graduated low and the percentage of the jobs from new starts rather than expansion high in absolute terms for rural enterprises in

Swaziland, but their differential performance gap compared to their urban counterparts was also particularly great (see Table 5.2). A poor agricultural performance in that country was apparently sufficient to outweigh a buoyant overall economic performance (1992 per capita GNP of $1,090 and annual GNP per capita growth from 1980 to 1992 of +1.61%).

These more macro agricultural economic indicators, however, still mask the ways in which the character and composition of agricultural growth affects the performance of rural enterprises. How does one explain, for example, the demand-driven expansion growth, albeit sometimes rather limited, that is taking place in all the surveyed countries, even in those with poor overall agricultural performances? One possible explanation is that some agricultural growth is taking place in certain localities or among farms of certain sizes. An illuminating example comes from a recent study that has examined how Malawi's decision in 1990 to permit smallholders to grow the major export crop, burley tobacco, might have affected rural non-farm enterprises (McPherson and Henry 1994). The study compared areas that now have large amounts of smallholder tobacco with closely paired control areas that had little or no smallholder production. The results show that existing MSEs in the smallholder burley-growing areas grew at an average annual rate of 8.8 percent since start-up, a rate that was significantly (statistically) higher than the 5.9 percent growth rate experienced in the control areas. Furthermore, the percentage of rural enterprise employment growth that came from enterprise expansion rather than from new start-ups was higher in the smallholder burley areas. The study also found that wage rates paid by rural enterprises in the smallholder burley areas grew at an annual rate of 34 percent, while those in the control areas grew at only 22 percent. Finally, there is evidence of a more rapid sectoral shift in the smallholder burley area towards the activities with higher productivity and profits, such as food and beverage retailing. These results are consistent with a smallholder, demand-driven pattern of enterprise growth (Haggblade and Liedholm 1991).

Enterprise dynamics by sector and by country

A second type of disaggregation of MSEs focuses on the sectoral dimension. The analysis presented in Chapter 3 has indicated that MSE survival and growth rates differed significantly by sector. In this section, these sectoral patterns will be examined in more detail.

Sectoral growth rates for the broadly defined sectors in the five core African countries, plus South Africa, are shown in Table 4.3. Manufacturing typically tends to exhibit the slowest growth rates, while

Table 4.3 Average annual growth rates (%) in MSE employment – by major sectors

Sector	*Botswana*	*Kenya*	*Lesotho*	*Malawi*	*South Africa*	*Swazi-land*	*Zimbabwe*
Food, beverage, and tobacco (31)	6.1	31	1.1	7.8	19.5	7.3	15.9
Textiles, wearing apparel, and leather products (32)	19.2	20	5.9	6.8	13.0	3.6	3.3
Wood and wood processing (33)	27.6	40	5.6	10.0	43.3	5.4	4.0
Fabricated metal production (38)	15.0	33	55.7	5.3	38.1	18.3	6.2
Total, manufacturing (3)	11.9	33	4.0	8.7	21.1	5.6	5.6
Retail trade (62)	11.4	28	9.6	11.7	25.1	7.6	11.9
Restaurants, hotels, and bars (63)	4.8	35	1.1	21.9	28.6	24.2	0.9
Total, trade (6)	10.0	28	9.0	12.0	25.6	7.6	11.6
Services (9)	15.0	33	9.1	13.7	21.9	9.8	16.5
Total, all enterprises	11.4	29	5.9	10.5	23.9	6.6	7.4

Sources: See Table 3.6.

services typically are found to be growing the fastest. Within manufacturing, wood products showed the highest growth in three countries, metal fabrication in two, and food processing in one. At this level of aggregation, there appears to be considerable diversity in the sectoral patterns of growth by country, and no consistent regularities appear.

What patterns emerge when the manufacturing activities are examined using a finer sectoral breakdown? Instead of analyzing the wood and wood processing as one category, for example, what happens when the major components of the category, such as grass, cane, and bamboo products, or woodworking, are examined separately?

In this section, two of these sectors will be examined to see what patterns emerge when they are analyzed using this finer breakdown. The categories selected for this more detailed examination are two of the "big three" sectors that dominate small manufacturing enterprises around the world: wood and forest products, and garments and textiles.[2]

The starting point for this analysis is Table 4.4. This table shows some major characteristics, presented in terms of sectoral aggregates, for all garments and textiles enterprises, all enterprises in forest-based activities, and (for comparative purposes) all MSE manufacturing enterprises, in the six countries of Southern and Eastern Africa. Among the points illustrated by these aggregated data are the following. These two sectors account for about half the enterprises and the employment in MSE manufacturing enterprises in the six countries under study. More than 90 percent of the forest products enterprises operate in rural areas, a higher percentage than for manufacturing as a whole. Garments are more widely dispersed, with over 40 percent of the enterprises in larger urban areas. For forest products, 80 percent of the workers are proprietors and unpaid family members, a percentage similar to all manufacturing enterprises taken together. For garment producers, this figure is even higher; close to 90 percent of the work force is made up of proprietors and unpaid family members.

About half the owners in forest products are women, similar to manufacturing as a whole. For garments, the figure is much higher (close to 90 percent). The share of the work force that is female is somewhat lower than the ownership share in each of these two sectors. Particularly in garments, only a small percentage of all enterprises grew. Expansion accounted for only about 12 percent of the total existing employment in garment enterprises, an unusually low figure. Expansion was somewhat more widespread among forest products enterprises, with almost a quarter of the enterprises growing and with expansion accounting for over 30 percent of all new jobs.

What happens to these patterns when the data are disaggregated into

Table 4.4 Employment characteristics: sectoral aggregates

	Forest products	*Garments & textiles*	*Total manufacturing*
Enterprises, total	315,518	287,721	1,202,819
Employment, total	605,952	437,113	1,903,938
Employment per enterprise	1.9	1.5	1.5
Cities	4.7%	42.3%	18.2%
Small towns	2.0%	7.1%	4.3%
Rural areas	93.3%	50.7%	77.4%
Proprietors	66.5%	79.9%	64.5%
Unpaid family	14.1%	9.2%	14.0%
Paid workers	13.7%	6.7%	17.4%
Trainees	5.7%	4.2%	4.1%
Female owners	50.7%	86.8%	48.5%
Female workers	38.2%	83.7%	51.3%
Percent that grew	23.4%	13.3%	17.8%
Av. workers added per ent. per annum	0.15	0.06	0.12
Av. workers added per ent. per annum among growers	0.51	0.47	0.58
Start-up jobs	68.4%	88.2%	75.2%
Expansion jobs	31.6%	11.8%	24.8%

Note: These data are for six countries: Botswana, Kenya, Lesotho, Malawi, Swaziland, and Zimbabwe. Information on enterprise growth was collected only in a supplementary questionnaire in Lesotho, so that country is not included in the bottom half of the table (the sections dealing with employment growth).

the major components of each of these two sectors? The comparable information for the components of the wood and forest products sector is shown in Table 4.5.[3] For this discussion, the sector has been broken into three major components. Woodworking includes carpentry and furniture making as well as the fabrication of building materials such as doors and windows. Grass, cane, and bamboo includes the making of baskets, mats, and other similar weaving activities based on grasses and cane. Other forest products includes sawmills, the production of coal and charcoal, and wood carving.

Woodworking enterprises are, on average, significantly larger than the other two; they account for 20 percent of the enterprises and a third of the employment in the sector. Grass, cane, and bamboo activities account for two-thirds of the enterprises but only about half the employment. The third category covers less than 15 percent of the enterprises and employment in the sector.

Table 4.5 Employment characteristics: forest products

	Wood-working	*Grass, cane & bamboo*	*Other forest products*	*Total*
Enterprises, total	62,663	207,570	45,285	315,518
Employment, total	199,946	319,340	86,666	605,952
Employment per enterprise	3.3	1.5	1.9	1.9
Cities	16.8%	1.5%	2.5%	4.7%
Small towns	5.6%	1.8%	2.3%	2.0%
Rural areas	77.7%	97.6%	95.2%	93.3%
Proprietors	49.7%	76.9%	66.7%	66.5%
Unpaid family	10.2%	18.4%	7.5%	14.1%
Paid workers	28.6%	1.5%	24.4%	13.7%
Trainees	11.5%	3.3%	1.3%	5.7%
Female owners	3.1%	75.5%	2.7%	50.7%
Female workers	1.6%	70.9%	2.0%	38.2%
Percent that grew	48.0%	16.7%	24.3%	23.4%
Av. workers added per ent. p.a.	0.42	0.09	0.09	0.15
Av. workers added per ent. p.a. among growers	0.88	0.45	0.29	0.51
Start-up jobs	44.5%	80.0%	81.9%	68.4%
Expansion jobs	55.5%	20.2%	18.1%	31.6%

Source: Survey data.

The contrast between woodworking enterprises and producers of grass, cane, and bamboo products comes out strongly in these figures. Among woodworking enterprises, nearly half had grown, and expansion jobs accounted for more than half the current labor force. Of the labor force, 40 percent was made up of paid workers and trainees. The overwhelming majority of owners and workers were males. While the majority of the enterprises operated in rural areas, 20 percent were in major cities and smaller urban locations.

In all these dimensions, grass, cane, and bamboo present quite a different picture. Virtually all producers were in rural areas. Well under 20 percent had grown at all, and expansion jobs accounted for only about 20 percent of the existing work force. Family members (working proprietors and unpaid family members working in the enterprise) accounted for over 95 percent of the labor force. Three-quarters of the owners and an almost similar share of the workers were women.

The third component of the sector, other forest products activities, was intermediate between the other two. Three-quarters of the work force was

Table 4.6 Employment characteristics: garments and textiles

	Dress-making & tailoring	*Knitting*	*Weaving*	*Other garments & textiles*	*Total, garments and textiles*
Enterprises, total	94,435	158,964	17,695	16,627	287,721
Employment, total	156,957	230,980	28,425	20,751	437,113
Employment per enterprise	1.7	1.5	1.6	1.2	1.5
Cities	42.7%	45.0%	10.8%	47.1%	42.3%
Small towns	8.3%	6.3%	6.5%	6.5%	7.1%
Rural areas	48.9%	48.7%	82.7%	46.3%	50.7%
Proprietors	68.4%	88.9%	68.5%	81.4%	79.9%
Unpaid family	8.5%	8.8%	19.5%	5.5%	9.2%
Paid workers	14.7%	1.2%	3.6%	12.1%	6.7%
Trainees	8.4%	1.0%	8.4%	1.1%	4.2%
Female owners	71.0%	98.7%	56.5%	95.1%	86.8%
Female workers	67.0%	97.5%	60.3%	88.0%	83.7%
Percent that grew	20.4%	11.8%	9.6%	5.1%	13.3%
Av. workers added per ent. p.a.	0.12	0.03	0.09	0.03	0.06
Av. workers added per ent. p.a. among growers	0.59	0.37	0.51	0.78	0.47
Start-up jobs	80.3%	94.0%	77.5%	97.1%	88.2%
Expansion jobs	19.7%	6.0%	22.5%	2.9%	11.8%

Source: Survey data.
Note: Dressmaking and tailoring is referred to as "wearing apparel production" in the Kenya data set. In Zimbabwe, knitting includes crocheting.

made up of family members; one-quarter of the enterprises had grown, but expansion jobs accounted for less than 20 percent of all jobs. Forty-five percent of the employment was in enterprises reflecting supply-push forces.

Table 4.6 presents a similar breakdown among small producers of garments and textile products. In this case, the disaggregation is into four components: dressmaking and tailoring; knitting and crocheting; weaving; and other garments and textiles. The first two of these are by far the most important. Knitting and crocheting account for over half the enterprises and employment in this sector, with dressmaking and tailoring accounting for an additional third; the remaining two categories together account for only about 10 percent of the activity of the sector. Knitting and crocheting is in many ways a languishing activity. Only 12 percent of the enterprises grew at all; 94 percent of the employment is in start-up jobs, which individuals establish primarily because there are bleak alternatives; 98 percent of the workers are proprietors and unpaid family members. Virtually all the owners and workers in the activity are females.

Dressmaking and tailoring enterprises offer a somewhat more dynamic picture in terms of patterns of enterprise structure and employment growth. Nearly a quarter of the workers are paid employees and trainees. A significantly higher percentage of all enterprises had grown, and expansion jobs made a somewhat bigger contribution to the work force (20 percent of all jobs resulted from expansions). For this category, as for knitting and crocheting, about half the enterprises operated in urban parts of the country, with the rest in rural areas.

This picture of dressmaking and tailoring enterprises takes on new dimensions when it is further disaggregated by country (see Table 4.7). Dressmaking and tailoring activities in Botswana and Kenya are significantly different from their counterparts in the other countries under study. These are enterprises that are dependent to a significant degree on paid workers and trainees (over 70 percent of the work force in Botswana, and 44 percent in Kenya). About half the enterprises in Botswana and over 40 percent of those in Kenya had grown; expansion jobs made a significant contribution to job creation in both countries. In Botswana, the country where the dressmaking and tailoring MSEs showed the most dynamism, the overwhelming majority of owners and workers were women; in Kenya these figures were somewhat lower.[4]

The examination of these two sectors indicates that, in some cases, there are strong differences between narrowly defined sectors that are common across countries. In other cases, these detailed sectoral differences vary from one country to another; country differences seem to be at least as important as differences between the narrowly defined sectors.

To examine these relationships in a more precise way, the same formal statistical methods used in Chapter 3 to identify the relationship between growth and the standard independent variables – age, initial size, location, country of the enterprise, along with the gender of the entrepreneur – were applied separately to the wood and forest products sector and the garments and textile sector, but with each of these sectors now specified in a disaggregated way.[5]

Two key findings emerge from this more disaggregated statistical analysis. First, for the wood and forest products sector, sectoral disaggregation is important. Specifically, the analysis reveals that woodworking firms are more likely to experience a higher growth rate than their counterparts in grass, cane, and bamboo products. However, the two other sectoral categories – other forest-based manufacturing and forest products trade – were

Table 4.7 Dressmaking and tailoring: country breakdown

	Botswana	*Kenya*	*Lesotho*	*Malawi*	*Swaziland*	*Zimbabwe*	*Total, tailoring & dressmaking*
Enterprises, total	2,569	16,915	5,279	12,768	3,127	53,776	94,435
Employment, total	10,277	31,158	7,858	18,603	6,131	82,930	156,957
Employment per enterprise	4.0	1.8	1.5	1.5	1.9	1.5	1.7
Cities	15.2%	26.3%	10.1%	23.6%	16.0%	58.5%	42.7%
Small towns	17.3%	19.5%	10.2%	4.9%	9.7%	4.4%	8.3%
Rural areas	67.5%	54.2%	79.6%	71.4%	74.3%	36.6%	48.9%
Proprietors	27.9%	51.8%	80.0%	68.7%	73.7%	78.2%	68.4%
Unpaid family	0.4%	4.1%	3.6%	8.0%	13.0%	11.4%	8.5%
Paidworkers	43.2%	21.7%	12.6%	17.4%	6.0%	8.8%	14.7%
Trainees	28.5%	22.4%	3.7%	5.9%	7.2%	1.6%	8.4%
Female owners	91.4%	58.0%	78.3%	17.9%	93.0%	84.8%	71.0%
Female workers	93.5%	50.4%	83.9%	10.4%	84.3%	79.8%	67.0%
Percent that grew	49.6%	42.7%	–	17.7%	21.5%	12.6%	20.4%
Av. workers added per ent. p.a.	0.39	0.27	–	0.16	0.10	0.05	0.12
Av. workers added per ent. p.a. among growers	0.89	0.58	–	0.93	0.47	0.50	0.59
Start-up jobs	54.4%	61.4%	–	83.3%	73.5%	90.4%	80.3%
Expansion jobs	45.6%	38.6%	–	16.7%	26.5%	9.6%	19.7%

Source: Survey data.

not statistically significant. This analysis reinforces the importance of disaggregating the broader (two-digit ISIC) forest manufacturing classification into at least three components – woodworking, grass cane, and bamboo, and other forest-based manufacturing. Second, for the garments and clothing sector, sectoral disaggregation proved not to be important. None of the more finely defined categories within the sector were statistically significant. Yet three of the five country variables were significant for the garments and clothing sector, while only one was significant for the wood and forest products sector. For garments and textiles, disaggregation by country was more important in understanding patterns of growth than separation by sector; for wood products, the opposite was the case.

There are several lessons to be learned from this sectoral and country disaggregation of small enterprises. It would be easy to conclude from a first look at forest-based and garments enterprises that these are among the least auspicious sectors for small-enterprise growth. In the aggregate, supply-push forces appear to dominate the garment and textiles producers; only a small percentage have grown in the past, and even those that grew have expanded only in small amounts. Forest products appear to have performed only marginally better in terms of each of these measures of growth.

Yet within each of these two sectors, there are components that appear to have performed well. In the case of forest products, one can see this from a sectoral disaggregation. In woodworking activities, one of the components of the forest products sector, in the five countries taken together, nearly half the enterprises had grown, and more than 80 percent appear to reflect market-based, demand-driven forces at work. In the case of garments and textiles, while some differences were apparent at a disaggregated sectoral level, these differences showed up much more strongly with a further separation by country; dressmakers and tailors in Botswana and Kenya stood out by virtue of their much more dynamic growth patterns.

Perhaps the major lesson to be learned here concerns the need to be careful about broad generalizations. One can get clues as to which types of activities have the best record in terms of past success by looking at cross-country patterns; but this needs to be done with some care, and to be treated only as a first indication of where to begin one's search. The disaggregation reminds us that there are good things happening in corners of otherwise bleak broader pictures. As long as one recognizes that one is dealing with exceptions to larger historical patterns, those exceptions may be as important in identifying growth niches as the major patterns themselves.

Growth by alternative patterns of market linkages

MSEs operate as participants in market systems. They often rely on others to supply them with inputs used in their economic activities, and they sell their output to buyers. In considering MSEs as participants in market systems, there are two dimensions of interest. One concerns the nature of the links that join producers back to the supply of inputs and forward to consumers of the products. A second and related question concerns the nature of the products or services they produce themselves, as opposed to those that they rely on other producers to supply. An example illustrates what is at issue here. A small carpenter might cut trees which he or she saws into boards, using these to make simple tables for sale to neighbors. In this case, the entrepreneur gathers the raw materials and undertakes all the steps of transformation to fashion them into finished products for sale to an individual who is the final consumer; this is a fully vertically integrated operation.

Alternatively (or perhaps subsequently), such an entrepreneur might choose to specialize, limiting the range of functions performed: buying logs cut by someone else (i.e. buying unprocessed inputs), or buying boards from a sawmill (buying semi-finished products as inputs). On the other side of the market, the entrepreneur may sell products to a merchant who handles the marketing, or he or she may produce semi-finished products for sale to other businesses that use them as inputs in their own production activity (e.g. selling doors and windows to builders).

As these examples suggest, alternative patterns of input procurement and of product marketing can reflect alternative degrees to which a small producer engages in a complete and vertically integrated production and distribution system, or chooses to specialize, focusing on a narrower range of functions and activities.

Enterprises that move towards a more specialized mode of operation are open to a new set of risks not borne by those that operate in a more vertically integrated fashion. Such producers must rely on other participants in the market to supply them with required inputs in a manner that is reliable in terms of quantities, qualities, timing, and price. On the output side, again, they must trust buyers to take delivery of their products and pay reasonable prices for them in a timely manner.

Along with the increased risk, however, come the potential advantages of specialization: the ability to concentrate on a limited range of activities yielding higher returns. Beyond this, selling to traders or other producers rather than only to neighbors opens up opportunities to sell in larger and more dynamic markets. In general, we might expect increased involvement in increasingly complex markets to be associated with higher rates of enterprise closure, but also with higher incomes and higher rates of growth among those enterprises that manage to survive.[6]

Survey data make it possible to test some of these ideas. Unfortunately, information on closed enterprises does not include patterns of marketing. For existing enterprises, however, more information is available.

Table 4.8 presents information from three countries (Malawi, Swaziland, and Zimbabwe) where similar questions were asked concerning patterns of purchasing of inputs as well as of marketing the products made. This analysis is limited to manufacturing enterprises, since different forces would be at work for traders or enterprises in service sectors.

Looking first at the aggregate figures in panel (a), the row totals tell us that over 96 percent of the enterprises sold primarily to individuals; selling either to traders or to other manufacturers was a relatively rare phenomenon. The column totals indicate that about a third of the enterprises make or gather their own inputs without reliance on the market. While a few buy unprocessed inputs which they transform in their own production process, the majority purchase primarily semi-finished or finished products for use in their manufacturing activities.

Our interest is primarily in the block set out in bold outlines in the table. Enterprises that are the most fully vertically integrated are in the north-west corner of this block: those that gather their own inputs, and that sell to individuals as final consumers. From that starting point, a movement to the right would involve increasing reliance on others for supplying or processing inputs; a movement downwards would imply increasing reliance on either traders or other manufacturers as purchasers of output, perhaps associated with further processing of the output by the producer.

Panels (b) and (c) of the table look at growth patterns among enterprises with different marketing arrangements. What can be learned from an examination of these data? Perhaps the clearest finding is that a substantially higher percentage of those enterprises that sell to traders have grown in the past, and their average growth rates have been substantially higher, compared to those producers that sell directly to individuals. This is the case for each pattern of input procurement, and for all enterprises taken together.

The comparison between those that sell to individuals and those that sell to manufacturers is more ambiguous. In each case, a higher percentage among those selling to manufacturing enterprises had grown; but average growth rates are sometimes lower. The cell of enterprises buying unprocessed inputs and selling to manufacturers is instructive. The figures in the table tell us that over half the enterprises in this cell had grown, but the average growth rate for enterprises in this category was virtually zero.

Table 4.8 Patterns of input procurement and output marketing

(a) Percent of all enterprises that are in the category

Sells to:	*Makes or gathers inputs*	*Buys unprocessed inputs*	*Buys semi-processed or finished inputs*	*Other sources of inputs*	*Total*
Individuals	32.8	4.9	51.3	7.6	96.6
Traders	0.6	0.1	1.0	0*	1.7
Manufacturers	0.1	0*	0.1	0*	0.3
Others	0.4	0*	1.0	0*	1.4
Total	33.9	5.1	53.4	7.7	100.0

Note: 0* = less than 0.1%.

(b) Percent of all in the category that had grown

Sells to:	*Makes or gathers inputs*	*Buys unprocessed inputs*	*Buys semi-processed or finished inputs*	*Other*	*Total*
Individuals	15	18	18	30	18
Traders	59	30	57	35	56
Manufacturers	18	53	27	33	23
Others	43	26	23	13	28
Total	16	18	19	30	19

(c) Average growth rate per year

Sells to:	*Makes or gathers inputs*	*Buys unprocessed inputs*	*Buys semi-processed or finished inputs*	*Other*	*Total*
Individuals	0.04	0.07	0.07	0.15	0.07
Traders	0.93	1.25	0.27	1.34	0.60
Manufacturers	−0.10	0.01	0.54	0.53	0.17
Others	0.26	0.26	1.00	0.05	0.04
Total	0.06	0.05	0.07	0.15	0.08

Note: These data refer to Malawi, Swaziland, and Zimbabwe.

This reflects the fact that, while many have grown, a significant number of others have declined in size since start-up. This reinforces the point made above, that increased reliance on intermediate buyers in the marketing system can open up new opportunities, but also introduces new risks for small enterprises.

The movement to the right in this table – shifting from gathering inputs to buying unprocessed to semi- or finished products – is also ambiguous in these data. There is no evidence here that such changes are associated with more dynamic growth patterns. It appears that where an enterprise sells its output is more significant in terms of its impact on growth patterns than how it obtains its inputs.

There are a number of different institutional arrangements by which MSEs can move beyond a direct sale of their output to final consumers. Each of these could be thought of as an approach enabling small producers to concentrate on aspects of the production process that they are able to do comparatively effectively, relying on others – to whom they are linked through the market – to undertake other functions where they are less skilled. Of particular importance here are the tasks of product design and product marketing, as well as the selection and procurement of inputs. Among the different types of market linkages operating along these lines are the following:[7]

1 *Subcontracting*, an arrangement whereby a subcontractor pays suppliers to produce a particular component, according to designs furnished by the enterprise placing the order. This component is then incorporated by the subcontractor in a finished product, which the subcontractor then sells to final consumers.

   Alternatively, the subcontractor may hire the supplier to provide a particular service. In this arrangement, the person giving the order – the subcontractor – handles issues of product design and of marketing. The subcontractor also generally specifies the inputs to be used, and will often either provide these or specify where they are to be obtained. Sometimes the enterprise giving the orders also helps with the capital needs of the supplier (e.g. by supplying the materials directly, thereby reducing the need for working capital by the supplier).

2 *Franchising*, an arrangement where a franchiser specifies a product or service to be produced by the franchisee according to specifications set by the franchiser. The franchiser generally specifies the inputs and the production technology to be used. Marketing is then the responsibility of the franchisee, but with guidance and advice from the franchiser.

3 *Flexible specialization*, an arrangement involving market-based relationships between independent enterprises, each specializing in different steps in the production process, linked together through arm's-length market transactions. In this type of arrangement, each participant in the system is responsible for his or her own input procurement, product design, and output marketing. The gains come primarily from the increased specialization and associated increase in productivity that can result when each producer narrows the range of tasks for which he or she is responsible. Often these gains are

associated with enterprise clustering (i.e. close physical proximity of the different enterprises linked through the market).

4 A *consortium* of enterprises, cooperating to sell their products in a particular market. Here all aspects of input procurement and production are done by the individual enterprise, while marketing is undertaken jointly.

Each of these alternative arrangements has advantages as well as disadvantages from the perspective of a small enterprise. Each requires particular skills and abilities while each can be seen as a means of overcoming particular limitations on the part of the participant. For present purposes, the point to emphasize is that these are alternative institutional arrangements designed to attain a particular goal: to enable small producers to participate in more dynamic markets, even in situations where they themselves have only limited skills that would restrict their ability to move beyond local markets. The contribution of such expanded market reach to enterprise growth is obvious in the figures presented in Table 4.8.

Growth by gender

Significant differences in the patterns of MSE growth have earlier been identified, based on the gender of the entrepreneur. In this section, these gender effects and the issues they raise will be scrutinized in greater detail. After a review of the static gender profile, the gender evidence on new starts and closures along with that on net expansion will be synthesized. Evidence on the relationship between the macroeconomy and gender-differentiated growth follows, along with a discussion of the implications of these findings for programs and policies.

Characteristics: a snapshot

Large numbers of MSEs are owned and operated by women. At least 45 percent of MSEs in each of our survey countries were female headed, and in four of the seven the majority were owned by females (see Table 1.1). Women, however, accounted for a somewhat smaller share of total MSE employment. This was due not only to the smaller size of female-headed MSEs, but also to the small percentage of females that were employed in male-headed firms.[8] The importance of women-owned MSEs as generators of women's employment is reflected in these findings. MSEs headed by women also tend to be concentrated in a relatively narrow band of sectors or activities. Downing and Daniels

(1992) have noted that women's enterprises are concentrated and dominant in a number of more traditional manufacturing activities such as beer brewing, knitting, dressmaking, crocheting, and grass and cane work, as well as in retail trading. Although data are scarce, there was some additional evidence to support the contention that profits generated by these types of activities were quite low. In Zimbabwe (Daniels 1994), for example, the five sectors in which most female-owned enterprises were concentrated were among the least profitable enterprise sectors in the country.[9] Finally, MSEs headed by women were more likely than their male counterparts to operate from the home; in the survey countries, for example, 45 percent of the female-headed and only 19 percent of the male-headed MSEs were home based. Since it is the home-based MSEs that tend to be hidden and overlooked, women owners of MSEs are more likely to be "invisible entrepreneurs" (Weidemann 1992). Our discussion in Chapter 3 also made clear that enterprises operating out of the home have performed relatively poorly in terms of growth characteristics. The fact that many of them operate from the home means that enterprises owned by women face particularly daunting challenges.

New starts and closures – gender disaggregated

A key finding from the survey data was that the new start rates for female-headed MSEs are substantially higher than those of male-headed firms. In the six core countries, the female rate was over 5 percentage points higher than the male rate, a pattern that held in each country as well (see Table 4.9). These findings suggest that the surprisingly high overall enterprise birth rates (20 percent or more) revealed earlier were being driven to a significant degree by the high rate of emergence of new female entrepreneurs.

What factors might explain these gender-differentiated MSE new start rates? One possible explanation centers on the nature of the sectoral concentration of female-headed enterprises. In Zimbabwe, for example, Daniels (1995) noted that the five sectors with the highest percentage of women entrepreneurs had the lowest capital and skill entry barriers, which allowed easy entry and may have contributed to high net entry rates and potential overcrowding.

Annual enterprise closure rates disaggregated by gender are rather scarce. In the Dominican Republic, the only country with the requisite information (Cabal 1995), annual closure rates for enterprises run by females (43.2 percent) were over three times those for male-headed MSEs

Table 4.9 Annual MSE new starts rate – by gender of entrepreneur (%)

Country	*Gender of proprietor*			
	Female	*Male*	*Joint*	*Overall*
Botswana	26.7	22.3	17.6	25.2
Kenya	24.3	18.8	17.8	21.2
Malawi	24.9	18.6	25.3	21.7
Swaziland	21.7	22.9	10.9	21.7
Zimbabwe	22.1	12.9	8.1	19.3
Dominican Republic	24.1	19.2	n.a.	20.6
Overall average	24.1	19.1	15.9	21.6

Source: Computed from individual country data. In each case, these figures are calculated using figures on enterprise births during the last full year preceding the survey. Averages are unweighted across the five countries. The category "joint" refers to enterprises with multiple owners including both males and females.

(13.2 percent). Thus, both MSE closure and net entry rates were higher for firms headed by females.

What reasons might have accounted for the higher closure rates of the enterprises operated by females? Was it because they were concentrated in sectors with high closure rates such as trading, or was it due to gender itself? The previously described analysis (see Chapter 3) of closure patterns of MSEs in Swaziland, Zimbabwe, and the Dominican Republic revealed that the probability of female-run enterprises closing during the following year, holding other effects constant, was approximately 50 percent higher than for those run by males. Thus, gender itself would seem to be a significant factor in determining enterprise closings. A large share of the closings of female-headed MSEs, however, was for personal rather than for business reasons. Indeed, when only the closings due to "business failure" were examined, the gender variable no longer proved to be significant. Thus, female proprietors were no more likely to close owing to business failures than their male counterparts, once the effects of all other variables were taken into account.

Net expansion – gender disaggregated

The annual average growth rates of surviving MSEs headed by females were substantially lower than those of their male-headed counterparts in all the survey countries (see Table 4.10). Excluding Kenya, an outlier with extremely high growth rates for both female and male enterprises, female-headed enterprises grew in a narrow band around 7 percent, while those with male owners grew in a similarly narrow band around 11 percent per year.

What factors might account for these dramatic and statistically different growth rates by gender? Sector is often considered to play an important role in explaining these differences. Downing and Daniels (1992), among others, have marshalled evidence to show that female-headed enterprises tend to be concentrated in those sectors where the smallest amount of enterprise growth is occurring. Indeed, the individual country surveys typically reveal that in many of the sectors with the highest growth rates of existing firms, such as construction, transport, and personal services, female ownership is minimal.

Yet even for firms within the same sector, there is evidence that female-headed enterprises typically grow less rapidly than their male counterparts. The figures in Table 4.10 indicate that, with two exceptions, enterprises owned by males grew more rapidly (or at the same rate) than those owned by females in the manufacturing (ISIC 3), trade (ISIC 6), and service (ISIC 9) sectors of the African countries surveyed.[10]

Yet the two exceptions, trading in Malawi and services in Swaziland, provide an important reminder that MSEs owned by women do not always grow less rapidly than their male counterparts. Moreover, in several countries, females were dominant in sectors that experienced among the highest growth rates. Textile manufacturing and textile trading in Zimbabwe and textile manufacturing in Botswana, which were all predominantly female, exhibited, for example, the highest employment growth rates.[11] These findings provide an important reminder that not all female MSEs are mired in low-growth sectors.

Sector alone cannot account for the gender growth rate differentials. Indeed, the previously described (Chapter 3) statistical analysis of the determinants of existing enterprise growth in Africa revealed that existing male-run enterprises grew more rapidly than those run by their female counterparts, even after controlling for the effects of sector and other important growth determinants.[12]

One of the reasons for the relatively slower average growth rate of existing female-headed firms was that fewer of them were expanding. As indicated in Table 7.2, only 15 percent of the female-headed enterprises expanded in the surveyed countries, while 25 percent of the male-headed firms grew. A similar pattern was found in each country individually. Among the female-headed enterprises that did expand, relatively few succeeded in "graduating" to the size category of firms with ten or more workers. Although, as noted earlier, the "graduation" rate of microenterprises in general was low (1.1 percent), the comparable rate for enterprises owned by females is even more minuscule. Indeed, the "graduation rate" of male-headed MSEs was eight times that of their female-headed counterparts (Liedholm and Mead 1994).

Table 4.10 Average annual growth rate – by gender of entrepreneur (%)

Country	*Sector – annual growth rate – linear*			
	Manufacture (ISIC 3)	*Trade (ISIC 6)*	*Service (ISIC 9)*	*All sectors*
Botswana				
Female	11	4	6	7
Male	11	11	38	12
Kenya				
Female	26	21	7	22
Male	32	27	21	32
Malawi				
Female	5	13	14	9
Male	12	11	14	12
Swaziland				
Female	5	7	13	6
Male	14	11	5	11
Zimbabwe				
Female	5	11	10	6
Male	8	14	20	10
Dominican Republic				
Female	3	7	4	6
Male	15	8	4	9

Source: Survey data.

What are the possible explanations for the gender effects on growth? Mentioned in the literature are such factors as the dual domestic and productive responsibilities of women, and possible differences in the business objective of females and males. Females, with their particular responsibilities for sustaining the family, may be more risk averse than their male counterparts and thus may be more likely to use any available funds for diversification into new activities rather than for the expansion of existing ones (Downing and Daniels 1992). Females may also be more prone to using business funds to meet household needs (Berger 1989).

The macroeconomy and MSEs: gender disaggregated

Recent survey findings have suggested that female-headed MSEs were more strongly affected by changes in the overall level of economic activity both in the short and in the longer run than their male counterparts. In the short run, women-owned MSEs have exhibited much more quarter-to-quarter volatility than those owned by males. The 1993–4 Jamaica Quarterly Panel Survey (Gustafson and Liedholm 1995) showed, for example, that employment in female-owned MSEs typically fluctuated by 10 percent every quarter, while employment in male-owned firms rarely changed by more than 5 percent.

In the longer run, there is at least some preliminary evidence of a gender-differentiated response of entry and closure rates to changes in the overall level of economic activity. The evidence of a strong inverse relationship between the net entry rate in low-return activities and the overall level of the economy was noted earlier in Chapter 3. Since female-headed enterprises tend to be concentrated in such activities, one would expect the net entry rates of female-headed MSEs to decrease as the economy increases. Correspondingly, one might expect the closure rate for such low-return, female-dominated activities to be directly related to the level of activity. As overall economic conditions improve, such low-return, survival-type activities become less crucial. Recent evidence from the Dominican Republic surveys provides some support for at least the latter contention. In 1992–3, a good year, the annual closure rate of female-headed MSEs was 42.3 percent, but only 13.2 percent for their male counterparts; for 1993–4, a bad year, the female closure rate plummeted to 29.7 percent, while the male rate remained virtually unchanged at 13.4 percent (Cabal 1995).

Implications

One of the important implications of the gender findings is that there are large numbers of potential female clients of MSE programs, but many have been overlooked because they are typically "invisible entrepreneurs" operating out of their homes. MSE programs must be aggressive in identifying and approaching female clients by actively seeking them out and penetrating the household, where the vast majority of such MSEs exist.

It is also important that the dynamic characteristics of female-headed MSEs be incorporated into the design and implementation of policy and projects. Large numbers of women-owned MSEs are concentrated in highly volatile, household-based, low-return activities where growth prospects are bleak. For many of these MSEs, careful consideration should be given to the types of financial and non-financial interventions particularly appropriate for the non-growing enterprises, a topic that will be examined in more detail in Chapter 7. For those female entrepreneurs that desire to expand more substantially, however, attention must be focused on growing and more lucrative product lines. The simple provision of working capital alone will typically prove to be insufficient unless the corresponding product markets, inputs, technology, and skills are also in place or made available.

Summary

A comparison of enterprise birth, survival, and growth rates in urban and rural areas shows the influence of agricultural performance on enterprise dynamics. In particular, patterns of rural MSE dynamics appear to be influenced by three sets of factors: the rate of growth of agricultural output, the state of the rural labor market, and the level of development of the transport and marketing system linking rural locations with more dynamic urban markets. While there were variations from country to country, growth rates in urban areas are generally substantially higher than those in rural areas.

A sectoral disaggregation of survey results shows that detailed breakdowns by sector and by country can be quite revealing. The main conclusion is that, even in situations that seem to present a gloomy overall picture, there are often subcomponents, either by sector or by country, that are doing well. Generalizations based on multi-country averages need to be treated only as first approximations.

A disaggregation by marketing patterns suggests that different patterns of sales of output appear to have a greater impact on enterprise performance than different ways of procuring inputs. Of those that sold to intermediaries (traders or manufacturers), a higher percentage grew, and their average growth rates were higher, compared to those selling directly to individuals. More complex marketing patterns open up opportunities for greater specialization, while exposing the enterprise to higher risks.

Enterprises owned by women have higher enterprise birth rates, higher closure rates, and lower growth rates than those with male owners. In part, this reflects the sectoral differences of enterprises by gender; but that is only a partial explanation, since these relationships also hold in multiple regression analysis that takes account of these sectoral differences. Other possible explanations include differing goals as well as other family responsibilities for women. Since enterprises owned by women often operate out of the home, special efforts are needed to locate them and to respond to their needs.

5 MSEs and the macroeconomy

MSEs make a major contribution to the total economy in the nations in which they operate. Conversely, the state of the overall economy has a significant impact on patterns of growth of MSEs. In this chapter, we set out the major dimensions of these interrelationships.

MSEs are a major source of new jobs. Survey data for the five Africa core countries, which are summarized in Table 5.1, suggest that the expansion in employment in MSEs absorbed close to 30 percent of the increase in population of working age. Since not everybody of working age is working or even seeking work, the contribution of MSEs to the absorption of new workers joining the labor force is substantially higher than this, over 40 percent.[1] In terms of secular patterns of growth, then, MSEs are the single most frequently chosen path for people entering the labor force and seeking to find a way of earning a living in these developing countries.

New MSE jobs come into being in two ways: through new business creation, and through the expansion of existing enterprises. The distinction between the two is important since in many cases the forces leading to the growth of employment are different. It is often also true that the quality of the jobs arising from these two sources is different.

A higher percentage of the new jobs arising from new start-ups reflect survival efforts by people with few options. While not always true, a significant proportion of new enterprise starts are driven by a necessity of finding any source of income, even those providing only minimal returns, in situations where few alternatives are available. As indicated in Chapters 3 and 4, a substantial share of new MSE starts are one-person enterprises concentrated in activities that are the easiest to get established, that is those with the lowest barriers to entry, with a consequent danger of overcrowding and resulting low returns. Chapter 3 has also made clear that closure rates are particularly high in the early years of a new enterprise, which means that the employment opportunities that

Table 5.1 Increases in population, labor force, and employment in MSEs – 1980–90 (all figures in thousands of people)

	Bots-wana	*Kenya*	*Malawi*	*Swazi-land*	*Zimb-abwe*	*Five countries together*
Increase in population of working age	187	3,658	1,214	99	1,578	6,736
Increase in labor force	125	2,939	792	61	942	4,859
Increase in employment in small enterprises	55	731	443	56	809	2,094

Source: Mead (1994a).

Notes: All figures are aggregates over ten years. For population of working age and labor force, source is UNDP and World Bank, *African Development Indicators*, 1992. Working age is defined as 15–64. The source specifies that "labor force" refers to the economically active population, which comprises "all persons of either gender who furnish the labor to produce economic goods and services, as defined by the UN system of national accounts…[this] should include all production and processing of primary products, whether for the market, for barter, or for own consumption; the production of all other goods and services for the market; and in the case of households that produce such goods and services for the markets, the corresponding production for own consumption" (p. 291). Data on employment in small enterprises are from the GEMINI surveys; for details, see notes to Table 5.2 below.

come into being as a result of new businesses being started are particularly at risk of being short lived.

New MSE jobs arising from an expansion of existing enterprises are more likely to reflect a response to an identified business opportunity. Entrepreneurs take on additional workers primarily because they have tried a particular pattern of doing business, have found a market, and would like to expand their participation in that market. Such a pattern of employment expansion in response to identified market opportunities is particularly likely to hold in cases where the added worker is a paid worker: the entrepreneur would take on an additional worker if there is a reasonable prospect of covering the added costs from additional sales revenues. This reasoning is less clear if the additional worker is an unpaid family member or a trainee.

Returns to labor in jobs resulting from an expansion of existing enterprises appear to be substantially higher than those arising from new business start-ups. A recently completed survey in Kenya provides estimates of net returns to labor in various types of MSEs. Looking at new jobs that came into being during the eighteen months previous to the survey, returns to labor in enterprises that had expanded their labor force during that period were more than twice the levels earned in enterprises established during those eighteen months (Daniels *et al.* 1995). This is consistent with our expectation that expansion jobs are not only more likely to endure but are also likely to provide higher incomes than those that result from new business starts. It is also consistent with the earlier-mentioned findings of the higher efficiency of MSEs with more than one worker.

Most of the new MSE jobs, however, come into being through people starting their own new businesses. This is shown in Table 5.2, which presents information on the sources of jobs in the five African core countries. Of the 4.3 million people working in MSEs in these countries at the time of the recent surveys, about 3.3 million of those positions – approximately three-quarters of the total – came into being when the enterprise itself was started. The remaining quarter were taken on as a result of an expansion of existing micro and small business, subsequent to their start-up.[2]

While the figures in the previous paragraph reflect long-term patterns of job creation, the patterns can be quite different over shorter periods of time. In particular, there is evidence that, when the overall economy is growing well, many MSEs are also thriving and expanding by adding to their work force. Under such circumstances, the majority of new jobs in MSEs result from an expansion of existing enterprises. In times of macroeconomic stagnation, by contrast, all enterprises – large as well as small – are under pressures to cut back on their levels of employment. But people must still eat. To sustain themselves, then, many people are pressed to start new enterprises, since there are few alternatives available to them. In such times, then, the majority of new jobs in MSEs come from new business starts.

Detailed data from the Dominican Republic support this description. In that country, Miguel Cabal (1995) followed patterns of change in microenterprises in several locations over two years. The first year was a period of dynamic growth in the economy; the second year was one of stagnation. The resulting pattern of employment growth among MSEs is shown in Table 5.3.

The impact of the macroeconomic conditions on patterns of employment growth is obvious. During good times, expanding employment in existing MSEs made a major contribution to employment growth, while more jobs were lost from firm closings than from new enterprises being started. The following year, when the economy was stagnant, existing enterprises were reducing their employment levels; employment growth from net new starts, by contrast, switched from negative to positive. It is interesting to note that the main difference between these two years in terms of net new start-ups comes not primarily from variations in birth rates but rather from closure rates, which were much higher in the first

Table 5.2 Increase in employment in small enterprises: new start-ups vs. expansions (in thousands)

	Botswana	*Kenya*	*Malawi*	*Swaziland*	*Zimbabwe*	*Five countries together*
1981–90						
Employment creation through new start-ups	40	554	351	43	629	1,618
	(73%)	(76%)	(79%)	(77%)	(78%)	(77%)
Total employment through expansion of existing enterprises	15	177	92	13	179	476
	(27%)	(24%)	(21%)	(23%)	(22%)	(23%)
Total employment creation in small enterprises	55	731	443	56	809	2,094
Total, all years						
Employment creation through new start-ups	75	1,410	817	63	948	3,313
	(75%)	(73%)	(81%)	(74%)	(81%)	(77%)
Employment creation through expansion of existing enterprises	25	534	193	22	226	1,000
	(25%)	(27%)	(19%)	(26%)	(19%)	(23%)
Total employment creation in small enterprises	100	1,944	1,010	85	1,174	4,313

Source: Mead (1994a).

Notes: The survey asked, for each enterprise, the year of start-up, employment at start-up, and employment as of the date of the survey. In the first part of the table (1981–90), the first row tells initial employment in all enterprises started during these ten years. The second row tells the increase in employment from start-up until the survey date for all enterprises started during this ten-year period. The third row is the sum of the first two rows. The second part of the table (all years) follows the same approach for all enterprises covered in the survey, no matter what their starting date.

All figures refer only to enterprises that survived up to the time of the survey. This means that employment in enterprises that were started in the past but subsequently ceased production are not included. Furthermore, for the 1981–90 section of the table, expansion during this decade of enterprises started in previous years is not included, but expansion during 1991 and 1992 of enterprises started during this decade are included in estimates of expansion. These imprecisions are forced on us by the fact that we do not know for any particular enterprise precisely when employment expanded – only how much it grew from start-up until the date of the survey.

Table 5.3 Patterns of employment growth: Dominican Republic (percent)

	Growth rate in GDP/p.c. (% per year)	*Percent change p.a. employment in MSEs*		
		From net new start-ups	*From expansion of existing enterprises*	*Total: net overall change in MSE employment*
Period of rapid economic growth				
Mar. 1992–Mar. 1993	5.5%	−1.7%	+12.4%	+10.8%
Period of slow economic growth				
Mar. 1993–Mar. 1994	0.5%	+1.7%	−3.2%	−1.5%

Source: Cabal (1995).

year, when the economy was doing well, than in the following year, when the economy was stagnant.

Furthermore, as indicated in Chapter 4, the biggest variations in closures are in enterprises owned by women. One possible explanation is that many of the enterprises run by women are activities yielding only low returns that the entrepreneur is glad to be able to close when circumstances in the family improve or when better options become available.

A recent study of patterns of change in employment and sales in Jamaica throws further light on this pattern (Gustafson and Liedholm 1995). The period covered by this study – from mid-1993 through the end of 1994 – was one of macroeconomic stagnation. It appears that real GDP per capita was constant or even declining during this period. The survey results, looking at a panel of existing enterprises to examine their changes over time, found an average decline in employment of nearly 20 percent, while average real sales per month dropped in these enterprises by an average of 35 percent. Microenterprise promotion programs found themselves operating in particularly hostile circumstances; the unfavorable macro environment resulted in substantial contraction in both employment and sales for the average enterprise.

A person running a program with the principal objective of helping existing enterprises to expand must be aware that, in good times, the economic environment is supporting his or her efforts. When the economy itself is stagnant, by contrast, it will be much more difficult for MSEs to grow, even with the best types of support.

The discussion of the previous point focused primarily on rates of growth of real GDP and how variations in aggregate growth rates can influence patterns of MSE growth. But there are other aspects of macroeconomic policy that also impinge on the growth prospects for MSEs. One key issue has to do with price stability. In countries where monetary and fiscal policies are not under control so prices are increasing rapidly, it is extremely difficult for small enterprises to plan for orderly real growth. High nominal interest rates – even if reasonable in real terms – introduce a major additional dimension of risk, which can be particularly daunting for nascent entrepreneurs.

A second important policy variable concerns the stability of the policy environment. Long-term growth requires an ability to plan for the future. If policy established today is likely to be countermanded by new directives or new interpretations tomorrow, it is difficult to adopt a long-term time horizon. Such planning is also made more difficult where fraud and corruption lead to additional uncertainty as to the interpretation of the law.

A third important dimension of policy concerns the issue of access: to imports and foreign exchange, to credit, to domestically produced intermediate inputs, and to markets. Governments set the rules in each of these areas. They can establish them in such a way as to facilitate access on the part of MSE entrepreneurs, or they can tilt the balance in favor of larger enterprises or the public sector.

A recent survey in Zimbabwe throws light on some aspects of this changing policy environment (Daniels 1994). Microenterprise surveys were done twice in that country: once in 1991, and again in 1993. The 1991 survey came at the conclusion of a two-year period when real GDP per capita was approximately stable. During the two years from 1991 to 1993, by contrast, the economy was facing the worst drought in a century; real GDP per capita declined by about 3 percent per year. During the latter period, furthermore, there was extensive liberalization of the economy; the inflation rate increased sharply, and nominal interest rates were increased to keep pace with inflation. As Table 5.4 shows, the problems reported by small businesses changed sharply over this two-year period. As a result of a liberalization of imports and the removal of domestic restrictions, transport problems were significantly alleviated, as were problems of access to tools, machinery, and equipment (many of which are imported). With the stresses of a drought-induced stagnant national economy, however, domestic markets were contracting. High inflation rates pushed up nominal interest rates, while access to raw materials and other inputs continued to be a serious problem for many. Again, these figures serve to remind us that the kinds of problems and constraints that small enterprises face can vary substantially as a result of both changes in macroeconomic circumstances (here influenced strongly by the weather) and by an evolving policy environment. An assistance organization offering one kind of help (e.g. management training, or short-term micro credit) might precisely fill the needs of the clients under one set of circumstances, but be totally inadequate to their needs at a different point in the evolution of the economy.

Other evidence of the influence of particular government policies on microenterprise growth comes from cross-country comparisons. Producers in Malawi and in Zimbabwe were seriously constrained by problems in obtaining raw materials: leather for small shoemakers, cloth for tailors, metals for small machine shops. In large part, these problems arose from the government's regulatory policies that gave priority to the needs of large businesses (see Mead and Kunjeku 1993). In Kenya, a significant number of enterprises faced problems of harassment by the government, sometimes in the form of bulldozing of their work place (see Parker with Torres 1994). Clearly, such policies and regulations have had a major deleterious effect on the growth of microenterprises in particular countries.

Rural MSEs are particularly affected by the state of the rural economy. Rural producers are often particularly isolated, and thereby closely linked to developments in their own locality. The degree to which this constrains the growth of rural MSEs depends primarily on three things:[3]

1 the rates and patterns of growth of agriculture, which is normally the main source of income in rural areas;
2 the nature of the labor market, which can generate additional income from wage employment, perhaps in nearby secondary towns, thereby creating additional demand for non-farm goods and services in rural

Table 5.4 Principal problem reported at the time of the survey: Zimbabwe (percent of respondents listing this as most serious problem)

	1991 survey	*1993 survey*
Marketing	17.8	27.5
Finance	12.6	22.7
Inputs	17.7	22.6
Tools/machinery	9.4	3.6
Transport	16.0	3.1
Government regulations	0.4	2.3
All others	10.1	6.5
Subtotal: percent reporting problems	84.0	88.3
No problems reported	16.0	11.7

Source: Daniels (1994: 50).

POLICIES

areas as well as reducing the pressures on people to engage in low-productivity producing and trading activities; and

3 the degree to which the rural economy is integrated with the rest of the country. This latter factor is strongly influenced by the effectiveness of the transport and trading system that links rural small producers with the outside world.

In those economies, particularly in Africa, where agriculture forms a large percentage of GDP, the pattern of rural MSE development closely mirrors the performance of agriculture. Given the desultory overall performance of the agriculture sector in many countries of Africa, it is not surprising that the majority of new MSE jobs in rural areas have come from new starts rather than from more productive, demand-pull expansion. Conversely, the percentage of new jobs from new starts or that resulted in "graduation" tended to be higher in those countries where agriculture did relatively well (Liedholm *et al.* 1994).

These considerations assume particular significance since the discussion of Chapter 4 makes clear that the majority of MSEs are in rural areas. Two principal implications follow. First, there are important things that can be done to stimulate the growth of rural non-agricultural MSEs that focus on either more dynamic agricultural growth or improved linkages between rural producers and developments in nearby towns and cities. Higher incomes in rural areas, whether from a dynamic agricultural sector or from wage employment, can create rural markets for the products and services supplied by MSEs; alternatively, improved transport and marketing systems can provide outlets for rural producers by linking them to more distant and more dynamic market centers.

Second and conversely, in the absence of either expanding rural incomes or effective links with the outside, rural non-farm enterprises will find it extremely difficult to expand their output, since they will be attempting to sell in isolated and slowly growing markets. In such circumstances, MSE credit programs or non-financial assistance may make possible some increases in enterprise income, but there are severe limits to how far such policies can go in raising either income or employment. Particularly in relatively isolated areas, rural MSEs cannot be the engine that pulls the rest of the rural economy forward; such a "bootstrap" approach to development ("lifting oneself by one's own bootstraps") is an approach that faces major limitations. In such situations, perhaps the most important thing one can do to encourage the growth of rural non-farm MSEs involves a concentration on a more dynamic agriculture and/or more effective transport, communications, and distribution systems.

Non-farm activities can also have important feedback effects in stimulating agricultural growth. There is evidence from West Africa and elsewhere that rural households use profits from non-agricultural activities to invest in agriculture, thereby raising the productivity of their farming activities (see Reardon *et al.* 1994; Liedholm and Kilby 1989). Since as much as 80 percent of rural household cash revenue comes from non-farm sources, and given the paucity of financial institutions, this has been a key source of investment funds not only for MSEs but also for farming activities as well. A key implication of this finding is that the growth of non-farm activities can have important multiplier effects in stimulating the growth of agricultural output.

The direct effects of government licensing and regulatory policies appear to be limited, both in constraining new starts and in discouraging MSE growth. The indirect effects are more subtle and more pervasive. Many MSEs get started and continue for some time to operate outside the law (see Joumard *et al.* 1992). When such enterprises are asked about their principal problems, issues of government controls and regulations are rarely mentioned as issues of serious concern (see Table 6.1).

Many of the problems that entrepreneurs do identify, however, have their roots in the regulatory environment: access to inputs, whether domestic (influenced by domestic marketing controls and policies towards local monopolies) or imports (affected by foreign exchange control systems); or access to capital (influenced by a host of regulations of the financial system). Such regulations are particularly significant in influencing the ability of microenterprises to grow. Since enterprise expansion often involves more complex interactions with other commercial entities (traders, manufacturers, service agencies, the government), the development of smoothly operating market systems can be an important determinant of enterprise growth. The government has a key role to play in establishing such market systems.

Two key implications arise from these considerations. First, regulatory issues are substantially more important for MSEs than is revealed simply by asking the entrepreneurs what their principal problems are. Many regulatory impacts operate in circuitous and indirect ways that only emerge based on more detailed analysis of patterns of production and trade.

Second, regulatory issues are substantially more important in their impact on the ability of enterprises to grow than in their effects on new enterprises seeking to get started or to survive. This is particularly significant since we have argued that jobs arising from enterprise expansion are more likely to endure, more likely to reflect market-based opportunities, and more likely to generate higher incomes than those resulting from new starts.

It is easy for those engaged in MSE programs to underestimate the significance of the macroeconomic context in which their clients operate. This can result in types of assistance being offered that are inappropriate to the needs of the clients; it can also lead to missed opportunities to deal in cost-effective ways with the most pressing constraints these enterprises face. Finally, it can lead to distorted evaluations of the effectiveness of different programs, either because the macro context was unusually unfavorable so even the best programs could not have succeeded, or because program evaluations are claiming credit for successful MSE growth when in fact the main explanation was overall growth that was carrying MSEs forward.

Summary

In recent years, approximately 40 percent of the increase in the labor force in developing countries have found work in MSEs. Most of these new "employment openings" – about three-quarters, taking good years and bad together – come into being through new businesses being established. The remaining quarter comes through an expansion of existing enterprises. While there are exceptions, it appears that employment openings that result from an expansion of existing enterprises are more likely to reflect a response to identified market opportunities. This means that they generally result in jobs that are more likely to survive and that generate higher returns, compared to those that arise as a result of new activities just getting under way.

Over shorter periods of time, the balance between "new start-up jobs" and "expansion jobs" is influenced by the state of the macroeconomy. In good times, a higher percentage of new MSE openings come from an expansion of existing businesses. When the macroeconomy is stagnant, by contrast, fewer businesses are expanding; there is increased pressure to start new enterprises, even in activities yielding low returns. These impacts of the macro context on MSE developments can result from natural factors (e.g. weather) or from policy (e.g. price stability, the regulatory environment). They can be particularly important in rural areas, where stagnant and isolated markets can make the prospects for healthy growth of MSEs particularly problematic.

6 Problems faced by MSEs

Efforts to promote the development of MSEs often involve helping entrepreneurs solve problems that constrain their growth. To do this effectively, it is helpful to know which are the most serious problems (the "binding constraints") that small enterprises face.

A full analysis of this question would involve developing a complex understanding of the directions in which a particular small enterprise might evolve and the things that are required to enable it to survive and to thrive. It is not possible to gain this kind of in-depth understanding for thousands of different small enterprises in diverse activities in several countries. Our survey-based approach is a much less ambitious one that involved asking a sample of enterprises about the problems that they face. The question was asked concerning problems faced at three different stages in the life of the enterprise: at the time of start-up; during any periods of growth; and at the time of the survey. These particular questions were posed in the five core African countries, Botswana, Kenya, Malawi, Swaziland, and Zimbabwe, and it is the survey findings from these countries that are described in this chapter.[1]

The survey-based approach needs to be kept in mind in interpreting the results. Entrepreneurs may have only a limited understanding of the difficulties they face. Inability to develop and introduce new product types can be seen as a problem of markets for the products they do make, for example, while inability to manage input procurement may appear to them as a shortage of working capital. Furthermore, respondents may tailor their answers to the things they think the interviewer wants to hear or is most likely to be able to provide. Finally, it should be kept in mind that this survey was administered only to existing enterprises; it tells little about problems that constrain others from starting new businesses.

The discussion of this chapter starts with an overview of perceived problems reported by the entrepreneurs at the time of the surveys. This is examined first in terms of an average across all the countries studied, then in terms of a breakdown for the individual countries. This is followed with a comparison of problems faced at three stages in the life of the enterprise (at start-up, during growth periods, and at the time of the survey). Problems are then examined by location of the enterprise (urban vs. rural) and by the gender of the entrepreneur. Finally, there is a disaggregation of problems by sector of the enterprise, looking at the four narrowly defined sectors examined in Chapter 4.

Overview of problems and country differences

A summary of perceived problems at the time of the survey, including a five-country average as well as details from each of the five core African countries, is presented in Table 6.1.[2] The responses indicate that three categories of problems were predominant in these countries: access to capital, problems of markets, and access to raw materials and intermediate inputs. The relative importance of these three varied from country to country. Access to inputs was the most important problem area in Malawi and Zimbabwe, but was much less serious in Botswana and Swaziland; in the latter two countries, access to credit was the predominant difficulty reported. Access to markets was identified as a serious issue for MSEs in each of the five countries examined here.

In all countries, access to working capital was far more widely reported as a problem than was access to fixed capital. The main problem areas included under the heading of "other capital," particularly in Kenya and in Swaziland (where the numbers were substantial), concerned problems resulting from bad debt associated with credit they had extended. For such enterprises, the main financing problem arose from too much credit given rather than from too little credit received. It is interesting to note that issues of government controls and regulations were rarely mentioned as the most important constraint facing small enterprises. As discussed in Chapter 5, this finding needs to be interpreted with some care. Access to raw materials, or to capital, is often constrained precisely because of government controls and regulations (Mead and Kunjeku 1993); furthermore, these surveys were administered to enterprises that had succeeded in overcoming any start-up hurdles established by the authorities. There is little evidence here, however, that government regulations were the binding constraint for most small enterprises.[3]

Problems by stages in the life of the MSE

Table 6.2 shows the principal problems reported at three different stages in the history of the enterprise: at start-up; during any periods of growth

Table 6.1 Principal problem at the time of the survey: total and country detail

	Botswana	*Kenya*	*Malawi*	*Swaziland*	*Zimbabwe*	*Average, all countries*
Percent reporting any problems	72.6	85.6	90.0	55.3	83.5	85.4
What was the most important problem? (Percent among those reporting any problem)						
Working capital	25.1	9.9	17.5	23.1	12.5	13.2
Fixed capital	3.1	4.0	2.7	3.0	4.0	3.7
Other capital	20.0	2.2	4.6	12.6	8.8	5.7
Capital, total	48.2	16.1	24.8	36.2	25.2	22.4
Markets	24.1	26.0	24.8	29.6	20.4	23.8
Tools, equipment and repairs	2.1	3.3	2.5	2.0	7.1	4.4
Raw materials, intermediate inputs	8.2	22.0	30.4	7.5	27.5	25.3
Inputs, total	10.3	25.3	32.9	9.5	34.6	29.7
Taxes	0	0.4	1.5	0.5	0.3	0.6
Licenses, registration	0	0.4	1.5	2.0	1.1	0.9
Zoning, location, movement regs	0	0	0.1	1.5	0.6	0.3
Other government regs	0	4.4	2.1	0	1.2	2.5
Total, government regs	0	5.1	5.3	4.0	3.1	4.3
Transport	7.2	4.8	4.8	5.0	4.8	4.9
Labor force	4.6	0.4	0.8	0.5	1.7	1.0
Other problems	5.6	22.3	6.6	12.6	10.1	13.8

Source: Survey data.

in the enterprise; and at the time of the survey. Looking first at a comparison between problems at start-up and problems at the time of the survey, it is apparent that capital is a more important issue for small enterprises that are just getting under way. This is particularly the case with problems of fixed capital. Among those that grew, credit became a less serious constraint, being replaced in part by difficulties in obtaining the tools and equipment required for their expansion. Problems with transport and with finding the required workers caused difficulties for some during growth phases. By the time of the survey, access to raw materials and intermediate inputs had become the single most important problem area. As indicated above, this was not true of all countries but was a serious problem in several. Again, it is striking that even during start-up years and periods of growth, government regulations and restrictions appear to have been a major concern for only a small minority of the respondents.

Problems by location of the MSE

For this analysis, each country is divided into three components: enterprises in major urban locations (with more than 20,000 people); those in rural towns (with populations of 2,000–20,000 people); and those located in rural enumeration areas (with less than 2,000 people). Problems faced by enterprises in these different localities are reported in Table 6.3.

Among the points that emerge from this locational disaggregation, the following stand out. Capital appears to have been less of a problem for small enterprises in rural areas, probably primarily reflecting the types of activities that are undertaken there (i.e. most of the activities operating in rural areas are ones that require less capital). Markets were seen as a problem everywhere, but were somewhat more of a constraint for rural producers than for their urban counterparts. Raw material difficulties were particularly significant for enterprises in intermediate-sized towns. As one would expect, government regulations were substantially more onerous in the major cities, although even there only 7 percent of the respondents cited this as their major difficulty.

Problems by gender of the entrepreneur

One of the striking findings of the MSE surveys was the general similarity in types of perceived main problems reported by male-owned and female-owned businesses (see Table 6.4). One often hears about the problems faced by women entrepreneurs in small enterprises in the Third World, and no doubt there are many such special problems, yet it may be worth emphasizing that, in broad outlines, the principal problems they face

Table 6.2 Principal problem by stage in the life cycle of the MSE

	At start-up	*During periods of growth**	*At the time of the survey*
Percent with problems	69.6	21.5	85.0
Percent with two or more problems	42.1	9.7	56.6
What was the most important problem? (Percent among those reporting any problem)			
Working capital	16.7	9.3	13.2
Fixed capital	12.3	2.8	3.7
Other capital	7.6	11.1	5.7
Capital, total	36.6	23.2	22.4
Markets	23.2	18.7	23.8
Tools, equip. & repairs	5.4	10.7	4.4
Raw materials, intermed. inputs	14.6	14.4	25.3
Inputs, total	20.0	25.1	29.7
Taxes	0.6	0.8	0.6
Licenses, registration	1.7	0	0.9
Zoning, location, movement regs	0.8	1.5	0.3
Other gov. regs	1.2	2.3	2.5
Total, gov. regs	4.4	4.7	4.3
Transport	2.7	6.0	4.9
Labor force	0.9	5.2	1.0
Other problems	12.1	16.9	13.8

Source: Survey data.
*Percent with one or more problems in this column are the percent of those that grew.

appear to be similar to those encountered by their male counterparts. Many of the major challenges facing those who start and run a small business are common to entrepreneurs of both genders. The primary problem cited by female entrepreneurs was not a lack of capital but an inadequate market demand, closely followed by lack of access to raw materials and intermediate inputs. Men, by contrast, complained somewhat more about their access to fixed and working capital, their access to tools and equipment, and constraints arising from government regulations. It is possible that these gender differences primarily reflect the particular activities in which female and male entrepreneurs are engaged.

Does this mean that credit is not a pressing need for women entrepreneurs? As discussed by Downing and Daniels (1992: 12),

Table 6.3 Principal problem at the time of the survey, by location of the MSE

	Major cities	*Secondary towns*	*Rural areas*
Percent with problems	82.2	84.4	83.9
What was the most important problem? (Percent of those reporting problems)			
Working capital	13.0	14.6	9.5
Fixed capital	5.6	3.6	1.9
Other capital	6.3	5.8	5.5
Capital, total	24.8	23.9	16.9
Markets	23.3	24.2	26.4
Tools, equipment and repairs	3.7	3.0	5.2
Raw materials, intermed. inputs	20.2	27.8	22.8
Inputs, total	23.8	30.7	28.0
Taxes	0.4	0.9	0.4
Licenses, registration	2.3	0.5	0.4
Zoning, location, movement regs	0.5	0.1	0
Other government regs	4.1	1.2	1.4
Total, government regs	7.2	2.6	2.2
Transport	8.5	3.6	9.4
Labor force	0.9	1.2	0.9
Other problems	11.5	13.8	16.0

Source: Survey data.

although women may cite insufficient working capital less often than men, this does not mean they have more access to working capital. It may indicate that women's market problems are more paramount. Without a market, they may have little viable use for financing.

Problems by subsector

In Chapter 4, the garments and textiles as well as the forest products sectors were separated into their principal components. In each case, one component (knitting and crocheting, in the garments sector, and grass, cane, and bamboo products, in forest products) appeared to be simpler in terms of skill and capital requirements. In each case, there was another principal component (tailoring and dressmaking, and woodworking) that was more demanding in both of these dimensions. Our goal in this section is to extend that discussion by looking at problems faced by enterprises in

Table 6.4 Principal problem at the time of the survey, by gender of the owner

	Female owners	*Male owners*
Percent with problems	80.6	88.7
What was the most important problem? (Percent among those reporting any problem)		
Working capital	12.7	14.6
Fixed capital	2.3	5.2
Other capital	7.7	4.0
Capital, total	22.6	23.7
Markets	26.7	21.6
Tools, equip. & repairs	1.7	7.4
Raw materials, intermed. inputs	27.4	23.1
Inputs, total	29.1	30.5
Taxes	0.3	1.1
Licenses, registration	0.7	0.9
Zoning, location, movement regs	0.1	0.5
Other gov. regs	1.9	2.7
Total, gov. regs	3.0	5.3
Transport	3.2	6.1
Labor force	0.8	1.2
Other problems	14.7	11.5

Source: Survey data.

these more finely separated sectoral categories. The results are presented in Table 6.5.

Looking first at the comparison between grass, cane and bamboo products, on the one hand, and woodworking on the other, some striking differences appear. First of all, a higher percentage of those engaged in woodworking reported any problems at all. Capital – particularly working capital – was viewed as a serious issue by those engaged in woodworking, while it was of negligible importance for those in grass, cane, and bamboo enterprises. Access to tools and equipment was likewise a more serious problem for woodworkers. For those engaged in activities making use of grass, cane, and bamboo, the most serious problem was reported to be one of markets, an issue of somewhat less importance for the woodworkers. It is surprising to find that government regulations were somewhat more of a problem for the simpler production lines in this sector. They also faced problems in their access to transport, complaining that public transport was expensive and unreliable. The

Table 6.5 Principal problem at the time of the survey: detailed subsectors

	Knitting & crocheting	*Tailoring & dressmaking*	*Grass, cane & bamboo*	*Wood-working*
Percent with problems	81.4	82.3	73.8	90.7
What was the most important problem? (Percent among those reporting any problem)				
Working capital	15.1	19.7	2.7	16.1
Fixed capital	1.1	5.0	1.6	7.7
Other capital	17.5	5.4	1.7	8.4
Capital, total	33.6	30.2	6.1	32.1
Markets	24.2	27.3	29.3	17.2
Tools, equip. & repairs	3.6	7.7	0	15.6
Raw materials, intermed. inputs	31.8	19.7	30.1	25.6
Inputs, total	35.4	27.4	30.1	41.2
Taxes	0	1.3	1.6	0
Licenses, registration	0	0	3.4	2.0
Zoning, location, movement regs	0	0	0	0
Other gov. regs	0	0.6	1.8	0.1
Total, gov. regs	0	1.8	6.7	2.1
Transport	1.0	1.2	11.9	2.1
Labor force	1.3	1.2	0.2	1.4
Other problems	4.6	10.7	15.5	3.9

Source: Survey data.

"other problems" for grass, cane, and bamboo were primarily among those facing personal problems (sickness etc.).

Turning to the other pair of activities, those engaged in garment and textile production, the differences are not as striking as those in the forest products activities. This corresponds with the finding in Chapter 4 that differences by country were found to be larger among garment producers than differences by narrowly defined sectors. One thing that does stand out in Table 6.5 is the substantial number of people facing problems under the heading of "other capital." This reflects problems of credit given and not repaid, reported to be a significant problem among knitters and crocheters in Malawi, Swaziland, and Zimbabwe.

Summary

When asked about the principal problems that constrain their development, entrepreneurs in all countries focus on three main areas: markets for the products they sell; access to inputs required to make these products; and finance. The relative emphasis between these three varied from country to country and from one subgroup to another within each country, but these three were consistently identified as the most important problem areas.

Looking at reported problems at various points in the life cycle of the enterprise, access to capital, particularly fixed capital, was especially problematic for enterprises just getting started. During periods of rapid growth, enterprises reported fewer serious problems on the whole. Identified problems at that stage included finding workers to meet the growing demands they were seeking to serve, and transport of their products to growing markets. Credit was less of an issue for rural enterprises, probably reflecting primarily the types of products being supplied (i.e. this reflects a lower demand, not a more adequate supply). There were only relatively minor differences between problems faced by male vs. female owners; the principal issues faced are common to both. While one must interpret this finding with caution, government regulations were reported to be of minor importance in all the disaggregations of the survey responses to this question.

7 The diverse characteristics and needs of MSEs

A review of the characteristics of MSEs confirms what all those working in the field know: this is an extremely diverse set of enterprises. Two points, central to this heterogeneity, have important implications for those responsible for designing and implementing MSE assistance programs. First, different types of MSEs have different contributions to make to the process of development. Some types of microenterprises are particularly effective in combating poverty, while others can make a major contribution in terms of economic growth.

Second, different categories of MSEs face different problems, and therefore can best be supported by different types of assistance. An understanding of these differences makes it possible to focus on appropriate categories of enterprises in offering assistance, and to offer support based on the needs of the particular types of clients selected for encouragement.

Building on the dynamic information presented in previous chapters, we have found it useful to examine MSEs in four major categories:

1 *New starts*. These are enterprises just getting under way. The needs of this group for support are significantly different from those of enterprises that have been in existence for some time and that have managed to overcome many of their start-up problems.
2 *Non-growing enterprises*. These are enterprises that have survived the perils of start-up but have not added to their employment since they were first established.
3 *Small growers*. These are enterprises that have been in existence for some time and have added to their work force since starting, but have grown only in small amounts.
4 *Graduates*. These are enterprises that started from a very small base and have made a transition to reach at least the middle ranges of the small enterprise spectrum.

The principal characteristics and problems of MSEs in these different categories are summarized in Tables 7.1–7.3. Our discussion examines these enterprise categories one by one, suggesting the characteristics of MSEs in each group, the goals and objectives that might be appropriate for the encouragement of each, and the project and policy implications.

New starts

A number of microenterprise assistance programs are targeted at MSEs just getting started. Many of these programs working with newly established enterprises focus on particular client groups: those that are specially vulnerable (low-income women, people in poor regions, etc.), or groups for whom the government feels a particular responsibility (retrenched civil servants, demobilized soldiers, etc.).

Two objectives are generally advanced for programs designed to provide assistance to these newly established enterprises: (1) *increase the rate of new start-ups*, eliminating barriers that hinder people from starting out in business; and (2) *help newly established enterprises to survive*, reducing the high attrition rate among those just getting under way.

In considering these programs and their objectives, one must start from several facts concerning this target group. Microenterprise new start rates are already high. Many people are already exercising an option of opening a new business. As we have seen in Chapter 3, new start rates of 20 percent or more per year are the norm in most of the countries with relevant data.

Moreover, for those that do get established, it does not appear that the legal and regulatory framework has been a serious hindrance to the establishment of most enterprises. In most countries, a substantial percentage start with little or no legal recognition; as indicated in Table 7.3, governmental restrictions are rarely mentioned among the most serious problems facing newly established enterprises. In most countries, it is unrealistic to think that the easing of registration requirements or the removal of other similar legal obstacles will result in a major increase in the number of new small enterprises getting started. On the other hand, a significant share of all newly established enterprises do not survive for long. As noted in Chapter 3, attrition rates are highest in the first few years. Efforts aimed at a reduction in these high failure rates among new start-ups might be more appropriate than a concentration on increasing the rate of new entrants to the world of microenterprises.

Programs designed to help people get started and to help more new businesses survive the early teething years face a number of particularly daunting challenges. These emergent business people must master a host

Table 7.1 Characteristics of MSEs: contribution to income and welfare

	New starts	*Non-growing enterprises*	*Enterprises experiencing small growth*	*Enterprises that had graduated*	*Total, all enterprises*
1 *Contribution to employment*					
Share of all existing enterprises	28.1%	42.8%	12.0%	0.6%	100%
Share of employment among existing enterprises	26.0%	27.7%	18.4%	5.1%	100%
Source of new employment over the long haul	80%	0%	10%	5%	100%
Av. no. of workers per enterprise	1.8	1.2	2.9	16.3	1.9
2 *Part-time or full-time activities?*					
Av. no. of months worked per year	10.6	10.9	11.2	10.7	10.9
Av. no. of days worked per month	23.3	24.2	25.4	24.8	24.3
3 *Contribution of MSE to household income (% of all respondents in category)*					
100% of hh income	30.7	35.6	34.0	21.7	33.7
50–99% of hh income	33.3	35.5	41.9	59.5	35.3
Less than 50% of hh income	36.0	28.9	24.2	18.7	31.0
4 *Contribution to distributional objectives*					
Percentage of female owners	56.9	60.4	38.5	8.4	54.2
Percentage of female workers	47.0	55.1	35.9	8.9	42.2
Percent of employment in rural areas	71.6	74.1	70.4	79.5	72.7

Source: Survey data.
Note: All data are from the six core countries (Botswana, Kenya, Malawi, Swaziland, Zimbabwe, and the Dominican Republic).

Table 7.2 Growth characteristics of microenterprises (percent distribution of all enterprises more than one year old that started with 1–4 workers)

	No growth	*Small growth*	*Graduates*	*Total*
All microenterprises	77.2	21.7	1.1	100.0
Female-owned enterprises	84.7	15.2	0.2	100.0
Male-owned enterprises	75.1	23.3	1.6	100.0
Manufacturing enterprises	88.5	10.7	0.8	100.0
Trade and commerce enterprises	76.2	23.5	0.4	100.0
Enterprises in urban areas	77.3	21.8	0.8	100.0
Enterprises in secondary towns	73.3	26.2	0.5	100.0
Enterprises in rural areas	77.5	21.3	1.2	100.0

Notes: This table refers to all enterprises that had been in existence for more than a year and that started with less than five workers. Those with missing data, those whose employment declined or grew by intermediate amounts are excluded from these statistics. These exclusions account for less than 5 percent of those covered by the surveys that started with less than five workers.

of new skills; their needs can be diverse and complex, which can substantially raise the cost of assisting them. High attrition rates reduce the returns derived from these efforts, since many of those that are helped will not survive for long in business.

Chances of success can be substantially increased if the assistance is channeled primarily to entrepreneurs who have had previous experience in that particular activity, perhaps having worked for someone else before starting a new business, so they will have been able to master at least some aspects of the business before they start out on their own. Building on previous experience in this way can raise the cost-effectiveness of assistance programs, since it decreases the range of new skills that an entrepreneur must master.

Efforts to strengthen the skill base for nascent entrepreneurs while building on existing skills has another important potential contribution: it can increase the share of new starts that are in activities yielding higher returns rather than simply flooding into product lines with the lowest barriers to entry, activities that may already have large numbers of participants selling in saturated markets.

For newly established enterprises, as for several other categories, the most serious problem reported by survey respondents was one of finding markets (see Table 6.3). Another frequently reported problem, particu-

Table 7.3 Principal problem at the time of the survey

	New starts	*Non-growing enterprises*	*Enterprises experiencing small growth*	*Enterprises that had graduated*	*Total, all enterprises*
Percent with no problems	11.2	8.7	5.5	2.3	9.2
What was the most important problem? (Percent of those reporting problems)					
Working capital	13.2	14.6	12.3	12.4	13.8
Fixed capital	2.6	5.7	6.5	0.1	4.8
Other capital	11.8	8.5	6.2	2.9	9.1
Capital, total	27.7	28.9	25.0	15.3	27.7
Markets	29.1	27.1	26.4	7.4	27.3
Inputs	26.6	25.1	21.6	42.4	25.5
Government regs	3.7	3.3	3.8	4.3	3.8
Other problems	12.0	15.7	23.2	30.7	15.8

Source: Survey data from Kenya, Malawi, and Zimbabwe.

larly for newly established enterprises, came from the fact that customers placed orders but then did not pick them up or pay for them. Categorized here under the heading of "other capital," this might be expressed as a problem of too much credit given, rather than too little credit received. Problems relating to access to raw materials and other intermediate inputs are also a frequent source of complaint.

With this diversity of reported problems, it may be unrealistic to think that raising the supply of any single missing ingredient will substantially raise the flow of new entrants to the microenterprise universe. While over 10 percent of them report that they face no problems, the high attrition rate among new start-ups means that this figure might best be interpreted as stating that they do not yet know what their most serious problems will be.

This reasoning suggests two approaches for projects aimed at newly established enterprises:

1 *Provide on-the-job training for potential new entrepreneurs*, before they start a new business. One useful approach might involve programs aimed at enabling nascent entrepreneurs to work for others for a period of time before starting out on their own. Such apprenticeships or on-the-job training can be invaluable in increasing the likelihood of success for new entrepreneurs. Programs of this type might involve wage subsidies, providing an incentive for larger enterprises to take on additional workers. The employer would be required to provide these new workers with on-the-job training which would increase their ability to start their own business, if they so desire.
2 *Build on existing skills*, whether derived from such on-the-job training or based on the entrepreneur's existing knowledge. Demobilized soldiers may already know about machinery repair, or may have experience as drivers; retrenched civil servants may have the skills required to learn to operate computers or to organize and manage private schools. It is important to identify and build on such existing skills, in preparing people for the challenging task of running their own small business.

Even with these efforts, the task of providing assistance to newly established businesses is not an easy one. This leads to two possible approaches that many project planners have adopted to deal with this challenge. One involves restricting assistance to entrepreneurs who have proven themselves by running a business for at least a year, getting through their early teething problems on their own.

Alternatively, some have chosen to offer assistance to newly established enterprises, but involve limiting such assistance to people who have had relevant experience before starting out on their own, perhaps having worked for others in the same product line. The need to direct scarce resources to places where they can be used most productively would provide a strong justification for some such restriction.

Non-growing MSEs

We have seen in our discussion of Chapter 3 that, of those enterprises that do manage to survive the difficult start-up years, most do not grow. Among the universe of existing enterprises, then, the largest category is made up of non-growing enterprises. In a number of countries with recent small-enterprise surveys, three-quarters of all enterprises that started with less than five workers had not added even one worker to their labor force between the time of start-up and the date of the survey (see Table 7.2). When measured in terms of employment, growth is the exception rather than the rule for MSEs.

As shown in Table 7.1, 60 percent of the proprietors and over half the workers in non-growing enterprises are women. Most of these businesses are full-time activities in the sense that they operate every day, all year around.

The great majority of these non-growing MSEs can be thought of as survival activities. Among the most important characteristics of such survival enterprises are the following: their very small size, averaging only about 1.2 workers per enterprise, with most consisting of only one person working alone;[1] their operation in ways that mingle resources used in the enterprise with other activities of the household; their almost exclusive reliance on family labor (nearly 95 percent of the non-growing enterprises rely exclusively on working proprietors and unpaid family members, making no use at all of paid employees); their simple management techniques; and the fact that many people participate in these activities, in spite of the fact that the incomes they generate are low and declining over time, because they have no better alternatives available to them. Close to 30 percent are strictly supplementary activities, providing less than half the household's income (see Table 7.1), but for another third, these enterprises are the sole source of income for the household. Many of these people are very poor.

Intervention strategies for these survival activities might concentrate on one or both of two objectives: (1) raising income for the one or two people who currently work in the enterprise; and/or (2) increasing the number of such enterprises that succeed in growing by taking on additional workers.

With respect to the first objective, there are a number of different programs that can contribute in important ways to a goal of raising income, even without necessarily changing the essential characteristics of these enterprises as very small, family-based activities. Such a goal can be pursued through efforts to reduce costs, by increasing the volume of sales, or by switching to product lines that yield higher returns. Both financial and non-financial assistance can contribute to each of these objectives. Table 7.4 gives examples of each type of intervention.

Each of these different types of intervention has the potential of raising incomes for those engaged in the enterprise. Because these interventions seek to reach the large numbers of microenterprises that are family based and that currently often provide only low levels of income, these are important and useful things that correspond well with a primary focus on poverty alleviation, a focus of many donors and non-governmental organizations active in this area.

On the other hand, there are clear limits to the kinds of gains that one can hope to achieve from these changes, so long as the enterprise continues to operate on a household basis, with simple management skills and marketing patterns. An appropriate second goal for non-growing enterprises, then, might be to increase the numbers of such enterprises that succeed in breaking out of this non-growing category.

As indicated above, only about a quarter of the enterprises that start out very small currently manage to increase their levels of employment. While not relevant or appropriate for all non-growing microenterprises –

Table 7.4 Assistance options and objectives to raise enterprise income among survivalist enterprises

Objective	*Financial assistance*	*Non-financial assistance*
Reduce costs	Lower interest rates on borrowed funds. More access to credit can make it possible to buy inputs in bulk, therefore at lower price	Better management or different production technology can mean lower costs per unit
Raise volume of sales	More access to credit can make it possible to purchase more inputs and thereby increase sales	Better marketing systems can open up access to larger markets
Switch to more productive product lines	New products may require more fixed or working capital	Product adaptation can help to serve a more profitable market

not all entrepreneurs wish to move on to a larger size – a goal of helping a larger number among those that do have that wish to move into the growth category is a worthwhile component of any MSE support program. This would involve helping them make a transition to a more sophisticated management and a more complex involvement in the market. Such an expansion – particularly if it is associated with the use of hired labor – is often a reflection of the fact that the enterprise is moving to the next higher plateau, where the opportunities for increases in income and welfare are substantially higher. The types of interventions that might contribute to this goal are discussed in the following section.

Small growth

The category of small growth is made up of those enterprises that start out very small and that subsequently grow in small amounts. For our empirical analysis, we have delineated the category as made of enterprises that started out with 1–4 workers and that have added 1–4 additional workers to their labor force since start-up. As indicated above, about a quarter of those that started out in this very small size range have managed to make this type of expansion. While over 60 percent of these small-growth enterprises continued to rely exclusively on family members and other unpaid workers, the remaining enterprises – nearly 40 percent of the small growers – had at least one paid employee. On average, these small-growth enterprises were more than twice the size of the non-growers, with an average of 2.9 workers per enterprise (compared to 1.2 for the non-growers).

Information generated from surveys in the six core countries clarifies a number of characteristics of these slowly growing enterprises (see Table 7.1). Compared to the non-growers, there is a decline in the share of enterprises with women as entrepreneurs, from 60 percent to below 40 percent. There is also a similar decline in the share of the work force that are women. A larger percentage of these enterprises are of major importance to household welfare, with over 75 percent contributing at least half of the household income. Data from a supplementary questionnaire in Kenya suggest a substantially higher percentage of entrepreneurs that selected the activity because it was viewed as having good economic prospects, with a correspondingly smaller percentage choosing it simply because it matched the family's constrained options (see Table 7.5). Fewer of the entrepreneurs had previously been unemployed, while a larger percentage had either run another business or had been employed in another enterprise. A higher percentage had received training since start-up, and a higher percentage were seeking opportunities for further

Table 7.5 Characteristics of microenterprises: contribution to self-confidence and empowerment of the individual (percent)

	Non-growing enterprise	*Enterprises with small growth*	*Enterprises that had graduated*	*Total, all enterprises*
1 *What did you do before starting this business?*				
Ran another business	13.1	18.6	9.3	14.8
Employed (wage work)	42.6	47.7	68.2	45.4
Unemployed	28.7	19.2	2.5	24.9
New entrant to labor force/just out of school	4.9	7.5	17.4	5.7
Other	10.7	7.0	2.8	9.2
2 *How was the business started?*				
Started from scratch	89.3	87.2	78.1	87.9
Purchased as a going concern	0.8	1.6	12.5	1.4
Inherited	5.3	6.5	6.3	6.1
Other	4.6	4.8	3.1	4.6
3 *Are you a member of a business association? (Percent answering yes; Swaziland data only)*	7.2%	21.8%	47.1%	10.7%

Source: Survey data.

training (see Table 7.6). All of these indicators suggest a higher skill level as well as a more commercial orientation for the entrepreneurs in this group, compared to the non-growers.

Table 7.3 presents information on the nature of the problems faced by these and other types of enterprises. Several points stand out as one moves to the right across this table. An increasing share of enterprises were able to identify problem areas causing them difficulties. As entrepreneurs become more active, they also become increasingly aware of the factors that hold them back from growing more; conversely, those that have grown at all are more likely to be ambitious in seeking to expand more.

A second idea reflected in Table 7.3 is that, as enterprises become more dynamic, more of their problems migrate to the "other" category. They find they must deal with problems of work space, of transport, of access to utilities (water, electricity, telephones), etc. What this suggests is a simple but important idea: more dynamic MSEs have changing and more complex needs that often cannot be met by assistance programs offering only one type of intervention.

For enterprises that are growing, the design of assistance programs becomes increasingly challenging. The number of potential clients becomes smaller, and these can frequently be geographically dispersed. At the same time, their assistance needs often become increasingly diverse and complex. Yet the most effective assistance projects are often specialized, offering particular, focused types of support. While these issues arise in the provision of assistance for the 20 percent of all MSEs that are growing at all, they arise with particular force for the 1 percent of small enterprises that are seeking to make the transition to the upper end of the MSE scale. Our discussion of the kinds of approaches that may be used to respond in a cost-effective way to these challenges are presented in the following section of this chapter.

Graduates

While only about 1 percent of all MSEs starting out very small succeed in "graduating" to an enterprise with ten or more workers, this is an important group since it provides substantial numbers of jobs, is a major source of today's intermediate enterprises, and is often most closely attuned to market opportunities. If enterprises that have grown in small amounts have a more commercial orientation than those that have not expanded their work force at all, those that have experienced significant growth are of particular interest, in that they are the entrepreneurs who have been most successful in identifying profitable market opportunities.

Table 7.6 Credit and training received (percent)

	New starts	*Non-growing enterprises*	*Enterprises experiencing small growth*	*Enterprises that had graduated*	*Total, all enterprises*
1 *What was the principal source of money to start the business? (Only most important source reported)*					
Household and personal savings	85.6	82.1	82.6	65.6	82.5
Loans from family and friends	2.0	4.0	2.8	12.5	3.5
Loans from formal financial institutions	2.2	1.9	2.4	6.2	2.4
Loans from moneylenders	3.7	3.8	2.8	0	3.4
Other sources of finance	6.4	6.9	6.9	15.7	7.2
2 *Have you received any credit since start-up?*					
No credit received	84.0	87.4	84.2	62.2	85.3
Loans from family and friends	10.8	8.5	7.1	12.0	8.7
Loans from formal financial institutions	1.6	1.2	3.6	2.5	2.2
Loans from moneylenders	0.9	0.9	1.1	0.3	0.9
Other sources of credit	1.3	0.8	1.6	22.8	1.3
3 *Have you received any training since start-up? (Percent responding "yes")*	11.7	14.0	22.5	31.3	16.4
4 *What type of training would you wish to receive?*					
Management training	24.9	21.4	29.2	16.7	24.3
Technical/production training	11.8	14.3	15.4	16.7	14.5
Training in marketing	14.4	13.3	13.0	16.7	13.4
Training in bookkeeping	8.1	7.6	9.6	16.7	8.3
Other, including "don't know"	13.3	18.3	13.5	0	6.6
None desired	27.5	24.8	19.3	33.3	22.9

Source: Survey data. *Notes*: Sections 1 and 3 refer to Botswana, Malawi, Swaziland, and Zimbabwe. Section 2 is for all five African core countries. Section 4 is from Botswana, Kenya and Malawi.

The movement from a very small starting size to an intermediate level is a challenging task. As we have indicated, the survey results suggest that only about 1 percent of all enterprises starting with 1–4 workers have succeeded in making a transition to employ at least ten people. Yet since each such enterprise adds substantial numbers of workers to its labor force, this group accounts for about a quarter of all new jobs that are created as a result of an expansion of existing enterprises.

Approaching the question from the other end of the process, among those enterprises currently employing 10–50 workers, about half started with less than five workers and subsequently grew. This means that, even though only a small percentage of the very small starts have made this transition, the process is important in providing a "seedbed" for a significant share of today's universe of medium-sized enterprises.

Based on the information from the six core countries, summarized in tables in this chapter, several characteristics of the graduates stand out. Like the other categories, these enterprises are likely to be full-time activities, operating approximately the same numbers of months per year and days per month as the other categories. But they are much less likely to be supplementary activities for the household; over 80 percent of the graduating enterprises contributed at least half of the household's income. They are much more likely to have been started by someone who previously worked as a paid employee rather than someone who was previously unemployed. As an approach to a country's unemployment problem, the encouragement of graduating enterprises makes its contribution primarily through the creation of new job openings in the form of paid employment rather than through an increase in employment among entrepreneurs.

While small traders are more likely to grow somewhat, small manufacturers are more likely to grow in substantial amounts. The sectoral breakdown of MSEs presented in Table 7.2 suggests that, while the likelihood of any growth at all is higher for traders than for manufacturing enterprises, the likelihood of graduation – small though it is for all microenterprises – is about twice as high for manufacturing enterprises, compared to that of traders.

Perhaps the most surprising finding about the regional variations reported in Table 7.2 is how little they differ. Enterprises operating in dispersed rural areas have virtually the same growth patterns as those in the major cities. Those in rural (secondary) towns – locations with 2,000–20,000 inhabitants – are somewhat more likely to grow at all, although somewhat less likely to grow in large amounts. In general, though, these figures suggest similar overall patterns of growth in rural and urban areas. The fact that most enterprises operate in rural areas (see

Chapter 1) reminds us of the importance of including the rural clients in the target group of assistance programs.

There is also evidence that more dynamic MSEs are involved in more complex marketing patterns. As one moves across these tables from non-growing enterprises to those growing in small amounts to those that graduate, one of the changes that takes place in the enterprise concerns more complex ways of interacting with the market. In part, this has to do with the sources of inputs: are they gathered or made directly by the household, or are they purchased on a commercial basis from others? It also has to do with patterns of selling of the output: selling directly to friends and neighbors who are final consumers, or selling to other businesses, either traders or manufacturers, who either use the product as an input to their activities or sell it themselves to other buyers.

A move towards more complex marketing patterns along either of these two lines involves the mastery of a range of new skills. It often requires more sophisticated cash management; it also means being able to meet the requirements of more demanding and discriminating buyers, who are able to shop around among various alternative sources of supply. For enterprises that are able to master these requirements, the more complex patterns have two distinct advantages. They enable the enterprise to specialize, focusing only on those functions that it performs best, thereby contributing to increases in efficiency and income. Furthermore, these changes enable the business to move beyond relatively slowly growing, localized markets to larger and more dynamic markets for their products and services. For isolated rural producers, such links make it possible for them to be linked to more dynamic and more distant markets. These same market linkages can also provide important information to producers as to which products are most in demand and how they must be made if they are to meet the customers' requirements.

Survey responses throw light on the significance of these changes in marketing patterns (see Table 7.7). In terms of our growth categories, the table suggests that while no-growth and small-growth enterprises both sell overwhelmingly directly to individuals, a significant share of the graduates have moved to a primary reliance on traders for their markets, while a few were selling to other manufacturers. The table also makes clear that a movement beyond sales directly to individuals is associated with a higher share of the enterprises that have expanded their work force, as well as a higher average growth rate in employment. A much higher percentage of enterprises selling primarily to traders had grown; on average, they had grown quite rapidly. Of the smaller group selling primarily to other manufacturers, the percentage that had grown was not very different from those selling to individuals, but the average growth rate was more than twice as high. Clearly the movement to more complex marketing patterns – difficult as these changes can be for a microenterprise to manage – has resulted in significantly higher performance in terms of employment growth.

Graduating MSEs appear to have mastered these more complex arrangements. As a result, they face fewer problems in finding markets for their products. Table 7.3 reflects the clear drop in the importance of markets as a principal constraint for the enterprises that have graduated.

More surprisingly, capital also appears to be a less widespread constraint for the more dynamic MSEs. The number of enterprises listing credit as their principal problem is substantially smaller for those that have graduated, compared to those that have grown only a little or not at all. Like the issue of markets, these entrepreneurs apparently have found ways of dealing with their credit needs, while other problems have come to the forefront: access to inputs, to utilities, to transport, and to work space, with the latter categorized in Table 7.3 under the heading "other problems."

It is sometimes argued that the process of graduation is inhibited by governmental rules and regulations. For example, Snodgrass and Biggs (1996) indicate that most governmental regulations fail to reach the microfirms; as these firms increase in size, however, they become more visible and more subject to governmental regulation, thus introducing a disincentive to expand beyond a certain threshold. Timberg (1978) noted the large number of Indian firms just below the size required for registration, while de Soto (1989) has described the high transactions costs associated with registration. Recent evidence from Africa, however, indi-

Table 7.7 Growth patterns and marketing arrangements for microenterprises

	Sells primarily to individuals	*Sells primarily to traders*	*Sells primarily to other manufacturers*
Percent of all enterprises in different growth categories			
No-growth enterprises	94.6	1.5	0.1
Small growth enterprises	94.7	4.0	0.2
Graduates	73.4	20.8	2.3
Percent of all enterprises in the category that had grown	18	56	23
Average growth rate in employment (percent per year)	7	60	17

Source: Survey data.

Notes: These data are based on surveys in Malawi, Swaziland, and Zimbabwe. The first three lines of this table would add horizontally to 100% were it not for a small residual category of sales to others, or enterprises with missing data.

cates that registration, taxes, and other government regulations have not inhibited the growth of enterprises in the countries studied (McPherson and Liedholm 1996, and Table 7.3).

The objectives for assistance programs as these relate to graduating enterprises can be expressed in terms that are broadly similar to those for small growers: (1) increase the pace of growth, for those that are engaged in such growth; and (2) open this avenue to increasing numbers of entrepreneurs, particularly those currently participating only to a limited degree.

The range of skills that an entrepreneur requires to enable him or her to manage these changes is complex. Unlike the simplicity of micro credit programs that can provide significant benefits by offering one thing to large numbers of low-income people, efforts to assist entrepreneurs seeking to grow more rapidly or to graduate must address a more complex set of needs. While the assistance needs become more diverse, the target group of potential clients becomes smaller, exacerbating the problem of cost-effectiveness for assistance programs designed with this client group in mind.

Table 7.3 indicates that working capital needs are of concern even for graduating enterprises, but these businesses generally require substantially more funds than are offered by micro credit schemes. That table as well as everything we know about the characteristics of these businesses and the challenges they face make clear that small amounts of credit alone will generally be quite inadequate to their needs.

One possible way of responding to the need on the part of the more complex enterprises for multi-faceted assistance is to focus on particular subsectors. Such a subsectoral specialization would enable assistance organizations to gain a deeper understanding of technological and management requirements as well as market structures and potential market niches that could be filled by growing enterprises.

A second strand of this search for cost-effectiveness in the encouragement of more complex growing enterprises involves working with and reinforcing the operations of the market. As enterprises grow in size and sophistication, an increasing share of their needs will be met on a commercial basis from other businesses specialized in accounting or bookkeeping, training, or marketing. Through a process of "buyer mentoring," enterprises placing orders can be expected to take some responsibility for working with suppliers, helping them to meet the buyer's requirements (see Grierson and Mead 1995). Assistance programs must be designed to promote and encourage these market-based relationships. As in the case of subsidized credit, providing such assistance on a free or heavily subsidized basis can be a serious hindrance to such developments.[2]

A third aspect of cost-effective programs for more dynamic enterprises involves attention to the macroeconomy. For those enterprises seeking to grow more rapidly, the policy environment becomes increasingly important. The government has a key role to play in establishing and enforcing the rules of operation of the market: who can participate, where they can operate, who has access to foreign exchange or to credit, and what happens when an enterprise does not fulfill a contract. The overall stability of the macroeconomic environment, as influenced by monetary policy and the fiscal balance of the government, the honesty with which procedures are followed and rules enforced, are all of great importance in setting a context in which small enterprises can thrive and grow. Unpredictable and arbitrary administration of policy makes it extraordinarily difficult to run a growing business, as does a high rate of inflation. Assistance programs operating in such circumstances face unusually difficult challenges.

A fourth aspect of cost-effective interventions is the recognition of the importance of "human capital." Many of the enterprises that succeed in growing in substantial amounts are run by entrepreneurs who have previously worked in that line of business for others, thereby mastering at least some aspects of the business. There appears to be an interaction between general education and business skills: those best able to derive benefits from their experience are those with education at least through the completion of primary school. These facts are significant in indicating the importance of providing both an appropriate educational system and opportunities for on-the-job training; they can also help target assistance to those entrepreneurs most likely to be able to take advantage of it.

It is a major challenge to seek to provide such assistance in a cost-effective way. For a program to be cost effective, it must first of all be effective: it must respond to the true needs of the enterprise, providing real benefits to those it seeks to help. In addition, however, it must provide that assistance in such a way that the benefits are commensurate with the costs of supplying them. Our discussion of approaches to the provision of such assistance is presented in the concluding chapter.

Summary

This chapter has explored the question of heterogeneity in the MSE universe, recognizing that different categories of enterprises have different contributions to make to the dual goals of poverty alleviation and of growth.

New Starts. At any point in time, about a quarter of all existing MSEs are less than one year old. While starting a new business is never easy, high birth rates remind us that, for many potential new entrepreneurs, the barriers have not been insurmountable. Yet survival rates among new starts are low, and teething problems are many. With limited resources available, many project planners have chosen to focus their efforts on enterprises that have managed to survive on their own for at least a year. Assistance in this area might well be focused on helping people to gain experience by working for others to gain experience before starting out on their own. Newly established enterprises have a substantially greater chance of success if they can build on such experience.

Non-growers. Most MSEs start out very small and subsequently do not grow, at least in terms of employment. Many of these are started by women; three-quarters are in rural areas. Very few of the owners had ever received any training or credit. While a number faced difficulties in obtaining working capital, the most frequently cited problems concerned access to markets, to raw materials, and to intermediate inputs. Programs can help increase the levels, the reliability, and the stability of incomes by helping to lower costs, by raising the volume of sales, and by encouraging a switch to more profitable product lines.

Small growers. About 20 percent of enterprises that survive their difficult early years manage to expand by taking on additional workers, although most grew only in small amounts. Compared to those that had not grown, a higher percentage of these growers had received some form of training (although not any more had received credit). Compared to those that had not grown, a higher percentage of the owners had previously either run another business or worked for someone else in the same line of work; fewer had previously been unemployed. All of these characteristics suggest that the owners of these enterprises have a more commercial, business-like approach to the enterprise.

Graduates. Those that started out very small but subsequently grew to the upper end of the MSE scale are of particular interest. Although only about 1 percent of those starting very small managed to make this transition, their substantial growth was an important source of new jobs, and particularly of jobs yielding higher incomes.

Assistance programs to help enterprises that are growing, whether in small amounts or through graduation to larger scale, face particular problems of cost-effectiveness. The client population is generally made up of relatively few enterprises, often dispersed, with increasingly complex and diverse needs. Possible responses include a subsector focus, a market-based orientation, attention to the macroeconomic context in which these enterprises operate, and the development of education and training programs to strengthen the human capital of those engaged in such enterprises.

8 Summary and implications

Summary

This study has identified a number of characteristics of MSEs and their growth patterns that have strong implications for the design of policies and programs to support the development of such enterprises. The key points emerging from the preceding discussion include the following.

There is much churning in the universe of MSEs. Many new enterprises are started each year, but many others also cease operation. While new start rates vary by sector and location as well as over time, there is an underlying positive net stream of new businesses feeding the universe of MSEs. Not all closures should be considered as failures, since in some cases entrepreneurs close one business in order to move on to a preferable economic opportunity. For many, however – particularly those that take place in the first few years of life of the enterprise (when closure rates are highest) – the closure does reflect the fact that the enterprise was earning only marginal returns or was even losing money, so the entrepreneur had no alternative but to cease operating the business.

Among those enterprises that survive, most do not grow in terms of employment. Of all new enterprises starting out at the very small end of the MSE size range, only about a quarter subsequently added to their work force. Of course many of the others may have gained in efficiency and taken other steps to increase the incomes of those who work in the enterprise, but in terms of employment, an expansion in the number of workers in the enterprise is the exception rather than the rule.

Among the remaining quarter that do expand their work force after start-up, most grow only in small amounts, adding only a few additional workers. The process of graduation whereby enterprises start out very small and subsequently move into the upper end of the small enterprise size range is a transition managed by only about 1 percent of those that start out very small.

Employment opportunities in MSEs increase in two different ways: as new businesses are started, and through the expansion of existing enterprises. The distinction between these two is important since there is reason to believe that jobs arising from an expansion of existing enterprises are more likely to reflect an entrepreneur's response to a business opportunity: more workers are taken on only when a market opportunity has been identified, based at least in part on the experience of the enterprise. While some new start-ups are clearly similar in orientation (especially in cases where the entrepreneur had previous experience working in a similar activity), a larger percentage of the new starts reflect the push of people who must find any source of income to keep themselves alive, rather than the pull of identified and profitable business opportunities.

Over the long haul, most MSE jobs come into existence through new starts; about three-quarters of all existing job openings in MSEs originally came into being in this way, with the remainder resulting from an expansion of existing enterprises. Over shorter time periods, the balance between these two sources of MSE employment can vary substantially. One of the strongest influences appears to be the state of the macroeconomy: when the economy as a whole is growing well, many MSEs are adding to their work force, while the pressure to start new businesses slackens. When the economy itself is growing more slowly, by contrast, the opposite forces are at work: many existing small enterprises are stable in size or perhaps even contracting, but a shortage of viable options increases the pressures on people to start new businesses, even if these generate only minimal returns.

Different types of MSEs face different kinds of constraints. This is not a world where one type of assistance can effectively meet the needs of all different types of MSEs. Our discussion focused on four different categories of enterprises:

1 *Newly established enterprises*, where the entrepreneur needs to master a whole range of new skills and where a principal challenge in the short run may be simply the survival of the business.
2 *Established enterprises that are not growing*, the majority of existing small businesses. A central goal here might be an increase in income for the entrepreneur and any associated workers, as well as ensuring that the enterprise is able to continue to survive.
3 *Established enterprises that are growing, but only slowly*. These enterprises are more commercial in their orientation than the non-growers; it may be more feasible to provide them with support

that will enable them to grow more rapidly and/or to increase their efficiency.

4 *Establishments that have graduated to the upper end of the small enterprise scale*. These are the success stories of the MSE world. Support for them will require more sophisticated interventions tailored to their more complex circumstances and needs.

These different types of MSEs have very different contributions to make to the dual objectives of poverty alleviation and growth. Newly established businesses as well as existing but non-growing enterprises are a vehicle through which large numbers of people seek to address problems of poverty. Policies and programs aimed at this target group can increase the likelihood that such enterprises can survive; they can also help those so engaged to earn somewhat higher levels of income. Assistance efforts focused on enterprises that have added to their labor force, by contrast, make their major contribution in the area of growth: not only increases in employment, but also in terms of more substantial increases in productivity and income.

Both these goals of poverty alleviation and growth of income and employment are justifiable and significant. Which of the two one chooses to emphasize has an important impact on the type of enterprise on which one needs to focus attention. This in turn has important implications with regard to the type of assistance that is most appropriate, since different categories of enterprises face different opportunities and constraints and therefore have different needs.

The majority of MSEs are owned and operated by women, but enterprises with women as owners are often quite different from those owned by men. In general, enterprises owned by women are smaller; they are more likely to be in trading rather than in manufacturing, and are less likely to grow than those with male owners. Special efforts are required, if women-owned businesses are to participate fully in the more dynamic aspects of MSE development.

The study has provided support for most of the hypotheses advanced at the start of our analysis about patterns of firm growth and survival. A posited inverse relationship was confirmed between growth and the dependent variables, age and initial size. Other variables such as sector, location, and gender were also found to be associated with patterns of growth. Support was also established for the role of these same variables in explaining enterprise closures or survival, but with one key exception. The posited inverse relationship between initial size and closure was not found; rather, smaller firms were found to be more likely to survive than their larger-scale counterparts, an important finding for those concerned with assistance to MSEs.

Implications

Different private voluntary organizations (PVOs) and non-governmental organizations (NGOs) have different goals and objectives in their work with MSEs, as do different donors. These goals can differ substantially: in the degree to which they focus on poverty alleviation (as opposed to growth), the degree of targeting of assistance towards particular groups (e.g. women, the rural population, people in certain localities), their faith in the reliability of market relationships, or their beliefs concerning the extent of intervention required to overcome the limitations of the market.

The information presented in this study helps to clarify the characteristics of different types of microenterprises, to enable those responsible for the design and implementation of projects to concentrate on types of enterprises that correspond most closely with their objectives. Surviving enterprises that have not grown, for example, are an appropriate target group for PVOs or donors with a particular focus on poverty alleviation. Enterprises that have expanded since start-up, and particularly those that have "graduated," are more appropriate to those with a growth focus, who may also pay particular attention to helping more of the non-growing enterprises to move over into the growth category.

These are not hard-and-fast separations into watertight compartments. Some enterprises have expanded in terms of income and productivity, even though their employment may not have grown; they clearly can contribute to a growth objective. Conversely, some enterprises have added only unpaid family members to their work force and continue to make their principal contribution in the area of poverty alleviation. For all of these reasons, it is helpful to think of different enterprises as being positioned along a set of multi-dimensional continuums involving complex patterns of growth of employment and income, as well as the various factors that contribute to these different outcomes. Placing enterprises in a few major categories based on their past growth patterns, as we have done here, is an attempt to find generalizations in what is without doubt a complex process. In broad outlines, we find that this separation has helped to clarify the principal contributions and requirements of different categories of enterprise.

Individual PVO/NGOs also each have particular approaches for their organization, including particular packages of assistance that they offer. Some provide credit, while others focus on technology, bookkeeping, marketing, or any of a range of other types of business support services.

Some offer more than one of these types of assistance, while others specialize by doing only one.

A PVO that offers only credit would generally not be interested in a recommendation that it stop offering credit and switch to management training. A more relevant question for such an organization might be whether it should add an additional function, such as management training, to supplement a credit program ("they can't make use of our credit unless we also give them advice on how to use it"), or whether an institution offering multiple types of assistance should drop one or more of these, or should set up management procedures to keep each activity separate, so they can be separately administered and costed. A related question might be: suppose one institution feels that its target group of MSE clients requires both credit and management training, while it offers only the latter. Can the organization find a working partnership with another institution that offers the credit, so their separate and specialized activities are coordinated and mutually reinforcing?

In a sense, these are administrative or structural, "second-tier" questions that have to do with delivery procedures for supplying assistance. But there is a prior set of "first-tier" questions: what types of assistance do different types of microenterprises need? Is it "enough" to provide entrepreneurs with one type of assistance (e.g. micro credit), all by itself, or would providing two types of assistance in a coordinated way be more effective? A principal objective of this study has been to summarize what is currently known about this question. As suggested in the previous discussion, an important part of the response must be one based on a disaggregation of the MSE universe.

New starts

The first category of MSEs identified in our earlier discussion was that of new starts. There are numerous programs all over the developing world that provide advice, training, and small amounts of credit to very low-income people, to help them get started in business. There are also many programs aimed at the simplification or elimination of legal and regulatory requirements that are presumed to discourage the establishment of such new businesses.

In view of the existing high enterprise birth rates, the high attrition rates in early years of an enterprise's life, the fact that most new small enterprises appear not to have been constrained by existing laws and regulations, and the multiple needs of these new businesses, this is a particularly problematic group for assistance programs. For those who wish to offer support to clients in this category, our discussion suggested two approaches: (1) concentrate on providing experience for those considering setting up a new business, before they start out on their own, by developing internships or on-the-job training programs; and (2) to the extent that one does seek to assist new start-ups, build on existing experience, both in terms of any training offered and in terms of the selection of particular enterprises to support.

The problematic nature of programs for the promotion of new businesses has meant that many project administrators and funding agencies have chosen to stay away from new starts, concentrating instead on enterprises that have managed to overcome their original teething problems by continuing in business for at least one year. In general, we find this approach to be appropriate and justified.

Non-growing businesses

This is the largest group of MSEs. While some of these enterprises generate higher returns, the majority are essentially survival activities. As such, they are a particularly appropriate target group for those donors and assistance organizations with a primary focus on poverty alleviation.

For non-growing enterprises, micro credit programs can provide important help, particularly in contributing to modest increases in incomes. There is a large group of MSEs that can be helped immensely if they can gain access to small amounts of credit, provided without any other complementary support, in ways that are easily accessible. This is the category of enterprises that have survived their early teething problems and whose main objective is often not primarily to expand by hiring additional workers but to provide higher and more reliable income for participating family members. Small amounts of credit can help this group in important ways: by reducing their costs, by enabling them to purchase their inputs in larger quantities, and by allowing them to purchase inputs (and therefore to operate) on a more regular basis. For this group of enterprises – and they constitute well over half of all existing MSEs – small amounts of credit can be of tremendous help, even without any other type of assistance.

While such micro credit programs are highly desirable, it is important to recognize their limitations. They do not respond to what many of these entrepreneurs running very small businesses describe as their most serious problems: expanding markets, and improved access to inputs. Survey results in several countries strongly suggest that, even for this large category of MSEs (those that have been in existence for some time and that have not grown), micro credit programs do not respond to many of the most serious challenges the entrepreneurs say they face. As reported in

Chapter 7, problems of access to credit are matched by corresponding concerns for issues of markets and availability of inputs, as their most pressing problems. Among their most serious problems are those in the area of markets: if they produced more, they would have a hard time finding people to buy the additional output. If credit programs lead to a reduction in costs, they can help such people raise incomes, even if the entrepreneur is not able to increase the level of sales, and that can be very useful. But there are severe limitations to how far such programs can carry the enterprise, unless they are also able to address their other constraints, in terms of their ability to sell more, and to have better access to required inputs.

One of the lessons emphasized by those working in the area of micro credit is that, for many very small businesses, having a safe and reliable place to save is at least as important as having improved access to loans. This is consistent with the information in Table 7.6, which reminds us that nearly 90 percent of all non-growing enterprises had never received any credit from anybody. For most such enterprises, the most important source of funding for the accumulation of fixed assets or for working capital is from their own savings. It is for this reason that such programs are often referred to as micro finance activities (i.e. including the development of savings facilities) rather than the more restrictive term of micro credit.

The central appeal of micro finance programs is not that they address the most serious problems of their clients; rather, it is that they clearly do help, and that we know how to offer that type of assistance to large numbers of clients, in a cost-effective way. A major challenge is to find equally cost-effective ways of addressing other, equally urgent, problems facing that same group of enterprises, particularly those relating to markets and the supply of inputs.

The most effective programs for dealing with non-financial needs of non-growing enterprises may be indirect ones. These entrepreneurs are frequently quite unsophisticated and widely dispersed. Training programs designed to upgrade their management skills have generally proven to provide only limited benefits while operating at high costs. Effective programs to address the non-financial needs of this group must operate primarily at a systems level: changing policies that affect large numbers of small producers, working indirectly through the supply of raw materials or other inputs, or establishing better marketing systems (perhaps through the activities of private traders), to enable dispersed small producers to link up with more dynamic segments of the market (Boomgard *et al.* 1992).

Growing businesses

In order to grow in terms of employment, productivity, and income, an enterprise must submit itself increasingly to the discipline of the market, in anticipation of the benefits that a closer alignment with markets can bring. This will necessitate a growing understanding of the market's requirements in terms of product types, quality, timeliness, and price. It also requires expanding knowledge about and mastery of improved production technologies, and a variety of associated management skills. The corresponding benefits include opportunities to specialize and to link the enterprise's fortunes to more rapidly growing segments of the market.

None of this is easy. Nor should a recognition of the complexity of the task facing aspiring entrepreneurs be taken as implying that any particular assistance organization should seek to provide training and assistance in all these areas, either to teach entrepreneurs to perform all of these functions or to seek to perform them on their behalf. This older model of enterprise development has been tried in the past and found to be severely wanting (see Kilby 1988). Our analysis leads us to suggest a substantially less ambitious program, one that we think has a better chance of providing cost-effective support for growing enterprises, whether they are seeking only to grow in small amounts or to graduate to substantially larger size. Our suggestions are at three levels: (1) the economy-wide level; (2) the sectoral level; and (3) the individual enterprise level.

At an economy-wide level, the macroeconomic context is particularly crucial to the expansion of productive microenterprises. The most dynamic periods of enterprise expansion are those when prices are stable and when the overall economy is growing at a respectable pace. Particularly in rural areas, a dynamic agriculture can make a very important contribution to the expansion of productive employment among rural MSEs (which, in most countries, constitute the majority of MSEs). Conversely, when the overall economy is distorted, heavily regulated, or stagnant, relatively little expansion takes place among existing MSEs. Even under such circumstances, there may still be a substantial increase in MSE employment, as a result of new enterprises being started, but in such circumstances of macroeconomic stagnation, these would primarily be in low-income, survivalist activities just getting started, rather than in the more productive expansion of existing enterprises.

National policies can also contribute in important ways to human capital formation. The survey results suggest that education beyond the primary level is associated with higher income levels in the MSEs the entrepreneurs operate, as well as with higher growth rates in employment

REGULATION

in these enterprises. An effective public education system that incorporates a respect for entrepreneurship, along with a public recognition and validation of apprenticeship and on-the-job training programs, can all make important contributions to the supply of potential and capable entrepreneurs.

The regulatory environment needs to avoid discriminating against MSEs in terms of their access to imports as well as to domestic raw materials, credit, and work space. Growing enterprises must have equitable access to the inputs they require for their production needs. Although MSEs rarely recognize government regulations as being the source of their most serious problems, the effects of such regulations can be indirect but significant. Tariff structures, licensing regulations, and marketing controls have frequently been used to channel available supplies to the public sector or to larger private firms, leaving MSEs severely disadvantaged (Haggblade *et al.* 1996; Joumard *et al.* 1992). The elimination of such controls can expand the opportunities for dynamic enterprises to grow.

In sum, the most important dimensions of policy support for MSEs come from macroeconomic stability, predictability, and transparency; from positive and healthy overall economic growth; and from widespread and equitable access to foreign exchange, to education, and to other domestic inputs such as credit and raw materials.

At a sectoral level, focusing assistance on particular subsectors can raise the effectiveness of support to growing enterprises. Selecting particular subsectors for attention can enable those providing the assistance to gain greater familiarity with problems and opportunities facing enterprises operating in the sector. This increased specialization on the part of assistance agencies can result in an improved ability to identify opportunities for product development based on a better understanding of market niches and market structures. It can also lead to more specialized knowledge about technological and management problems and their solutions.

Many of the most successful efforts in the promotion of growing enterprises have been aimed at developing commercial, market-based linkages between independent enterprises. Many types of enterprise competence can be purchased in the market; this should be encouraged and facilitated, not stifled and undercut through subsidized (and often less competent) provision of the same services by government agencies or NGOs. In the same vein, vertical commercial linkages between independent enterprises can enable small enterprises to specialize in those functions that they perform best. Effective assistance programs can contribute to the spread of such market-based linkages (Grierson *et al.* 1997).

There has been considerable interest in recent years in the advantages to be derived by MSEs from cooperation to improve their operations by working together. It is claimed that cooperating along several lines can result in lower costs, higher sales, and an improved enterprise environment. This cooperation can come in several different domains: (1) performing certain functions jointly, such as purchasing inputs or selling products; (2) sharing information about best practices, about market opportunities or raw material sources; (3) mutual help in dealing with breakdowns, emergencies, or demands that temporarily exceed the capacity of one firm; and (4) lobbying to bring about changes in regulations or policies.

In the past, such arguments have often led to a suggestion for the promotion of cooperatives or of business associations. In spite of their obvious appeal, each of these institutional arrangements has had a checkered past in developing countries, primarily because they have often been promoted in a heavy-handed, "top-down" manner. The world in which MSEs operate is often a highly competitive one, where the level of trust between separate entrepreneurs has been low; efforts by the government or other outside agencies to preach the advantages of cooperation have been met with considerable skepticism, while attempts to press people into associations or cooperative arrangements have often been counterproductive.

The most recent incarnation in this area of interest has fallen under the heading of clusters. A number of analysts have argued that these geographical concentrations of enterprises in related activities have provided significant benefits to those who participate in them (Van Dijk and Rabellotti 1997; McCormick and Pedersen 1996; Schmitz 1995). While we recognize the great advantages that some enterprises have derived from such networks, particularly in developed countries (e.g. Italy) but also sometimes in developing countries (e.g. Brazil, India), we have seen little evidence of the advantages of such networks in our survey results;[1] nor have we found it to be very easy to promote their establishment in new locations in the Third World.

Moving on to issues that arise at an individual enterprise level, our experience leads us to believe that direct assistance should be focused and short term, of a problem-solving nature. There is often a tendency to think in terms of long-term relationships, providing training and advice over a period of several months or even years. Such longer-term, hand-holding programs can be very expensive, often produce only limited results, and frequently involve problems of long-term dependence on the assistance provider. Cost-effective programs are more likely to be built around offering specific answers to specific problems, with a short turnaround, enabling the assistance agency to provide only the help that is needed, but to a large number of clients.

A major part of such assistance might involve referrals: to commercial agencies able to provide the assistance for a fee, or to existing institutions or organizations specialized in the provision of such assistance, perhaps on a subsidized basis. Most countries already have an array of technology institutes, training programs, and commercial organizations, often each operating well below capacity, that would be willing and indeed eager to participate in networks seeking to respond to particular problems of growing businesses. Even if these have sometimes been less effective than one would hope, the best strategy is often one of working with existing structures to strengthen them through informed referrals, perhaps working with them to assist them in making their assistance more focused on helping entrepreneurs respond to identified needs and opportunities. Such an approach working with existing organizations appears to have a much greater chance of success – and, particularly, of being cost effective – than seeking to rebuild the whole structure through the establishment of new assistance organizations and programs.

There is no one right way to do microenterprise development. There are lots of wrong ways: in providing assistance that does not really help, or in providing help that is useful but is very expensive, and that therefore cannot be generalized or sustained and that gets in the way of developments that could provide assistance to more people.

The main message of this study may be a recognition of complexity and diversity in the MSE universe. There are different types of enterprises that have different valid and important contributions to make to the development process, that face different needs and can be helped in different ways. The design of effective policies and programs must be built on an understanding of that complexity. It is hoped that this study will contribute to that understanding.

Notes

1 Introduction

1 Included in this static profile are the six core countries where several dynamic MSE surveys were undertaken – Botswana, Kenya, Malawi, Swaziland, Zimbabwe, and the Dominican Republic – plus two others where baseline surveys were conducted – Lesotho and South Africa (two townships). For details, see Chapter 2. See also Liedholm and Mead (1987, 1994) and Snodgrass and Biggs (1996).
2 These figures refer to Botswana, Kenya, Malawi, Swaziland, and Zimbabwe. For details, see Mead (1994a).
3 This means that the analysis of dynamic patterns in this study is heavily influenced by those enterprises at the small end of the size spectrum. At various points of the analysis that follows, we examine the importance of size as a determinant of different aspects of growth, as well as focusing on different size-based categories of enterprises from this heterogeneous universe of MSEs.
4 Liedholm and Mead (1987).
5 Daniels *et al.* (1995).
6 As indicated in the discussion of Chapter 7, for some purposes we find it helpful to group together the second and third of these categories ("no-growth" and "small-growth" enterprises). With that modification, our categorization is quite similar to that of the US Agency for International Development, in its formulation of strategies for sustainable development. In relation to microenterprise and small business development, USAID states that its programs will

> address three elements that are critical to broad-based economic growth and participation: removing obstacles that impede the creation of new businesses that provide incomes; helping existing enterprises to expand; and supporting the transition of small businesses and microenterprises to the formal sector. (USAID 1994)

Our formulation in Chapter 7 is quite similar to this three-part focus.

2 MSE dynamics: theory and literature review

1 See Appendix A of Liedholm and Mead (1991) for more details.

2 See below for a discussion of issues of measurement for firm birth and death rates.
3 See Haggblade and Liedholm's (1991) model of the rural economy for an elaboration of these points.
4 See Liedholm and Mead (1987) for cross-section evidence and Parker (1994) and Parker *et al.* (1995) for time series evidence.
5 This is a sample censoring problem that can arise when a firm is born and then dies between the two survey periods. Such a firm would not be picked up by the panel survey and both its birth and death would go unrecorded.

3 New starts, closures, and expansion of MSEs

1 New start (birth) rates are typically calculated by dividing all new firms appearing in a given time period (usually one year) by the number of firms in existence at the beginning of the year. Except for the Dominican Republic, the number of firms at the end of the year served as the base; given the net increase in the number of firms, this creates one source of downward bias. A second source of downward bias, present in all countries, is the omission of the short-lived firms that appear and then disappear within the year. A study of short-lived firms in the Dominican Republic indicates that if these are included in the analysis, the birth rate in the Dominican Republic would have increased by 6.5 percentage points. For more details of these methodological issues, see Liedholm and Mead (1994).
2 Specifically, on the basis of area-based panel surveys, the annual closure rate was 29 percent in 1992 and 22 percent in 1993 (Cabal 1995). In Zimbabwe, a closure rate of 11.5 percent per year (from 1991 to 1993) was reported from a similar area-based panel survey of MSEs (Daniels 1995). However, 42 percent of the firms could not be located in the resurvey, so this closure rate must be considered a lower-bound estimate. Area-based panel surveys, where all enterprises in the same areas are surveyed over time, generate much more accurate closure rates than those generated from either tracer or closed enterprise surveys, both of which are subject to severe selectivity biases that understate the closure rates. Annual closure rates derived from tracer surveys range from 1.3 in Nigeria (Kilby 1994) to 4.1 percent in Jamaica (Fisseha 1994), while those from closed enterprise surveys hover around 6 percent per year.
3 In Kenya (Parker 1994), those who closed for demand reasons were much more likely to start a new enterprise than those who closed because of a lack of working capital. Indeed, overall, of those who closed, 60 percent subsequently opened new business, 15 percent worked in agriculture, 8 percent accepted paid employment, and 17 percent were no longer economically active.
4 This may be partially a function of when during the year the survey was undertaken.
5 The hazard analysis is more attractive than other statistical techniques for examining such patterns, because it not only permits time-varying explanatory variables to be included in the analysis, but also deals with the sample censoring problem that arises because not all the firms in the data set have closed. The observations about them are thus incomplete and these observations are called "censored." Standard econometric analyses, such as ordinary least squares, ignore this fact and count these firms as if they had closed and thus yield results that would be quite misleading. Hazard analysis, on the other

hand, only included information on those firms that are at risk of failing. The "hazard rate" is defined as the probability that the firm will close during the period, usually one year, given that it has survived until the beginning of the period. It is computed by dividing the number of firms that closed in a period by the number of those firms that have not yet closed at the beginning of the period. For more details see Liedholm and Mead (1993), or Allison (1984).

6 In the Dominican Republic, however, this relationship was not significant (Cabal 1995).

7 The complete sector ranking of MSEs by survival probabilities from highest to lowest in Swaziland and Zimbabwe combined was as follows: real estate, wood processing, wholesale trade, non-metallic minerals, textiles, other services, food and beverage processing, construction, miscellaneous manufacturing, metal fabrication, hotels and restaurants, chemicals, retail trade, and transport. The rank differences, however, were not always statistically significant (McPherson 1992).

8 The rural–urban distinction, however, was not statistically significant in the Dominican Republic (Cabal 1995).

9 Using regression analysis, Daniels (1995) found an inverse relationship between the GDP growth rate over the 1988–93 period and the annual closure rate in Zimbabwe.

10 The compound growth measure provides a lower-bound estimate of the growth rate compared to the average growth rate measure, which uses initial employment as the base. An absolute measure, the annual change in jobs per firm, is also presented in Table 3.6; it can be particularly useful in assessing the overall contribution of the smallest firms to job creation. The data for all the growth measures were generated by asking entrepreneurs retrospective information (event histories) about their firms.

11 About 5 percent of the enterprises had declined in size since start-up (see Liedholm and Mead 1994).

12 See Chapter 1 above as well as Liedholm and Mead (1987), for cross-section evidence. See Parker (1994), and Parker *et al.* (1995), for time series evidence.

13 Linear ordinary least-squares analysis was used to estimate and test the statistical relationships between the dependent and independent variables. Using the "Heckit" technique, it was also determined that the possible selectivity bias arising from examining only surviving firms in the analysis was not significant. Variables were reported significant at the 1 percent level. For details, see Liedholm and Mead (1994).

14 As Parker (1994) has shown, this finding needs to be qualified with the recognition that enterprises that start with one person cannot contract and still remain as an on-going enterprise. For larger enterprises, the fact that growth in some was offset by contraction in others is a partial explanation for the lower average growth rate for enterprises starting at a larger size.

15 No significant relationship between secondary school education and MSE expansion, however, could be found in Botswana or Swaziland (McPherson 1995).

4 MSE growth by location, sector, linkages, and gender

1 The results from these two countries, Zimbabwe and Malawi, are similar to the earlier new start findings reported for Sierra Leone (Chuta and Liedholm

1985), where the annual birth rate in urban areas was 14.9 percent and that in the rural enumeration areas was only 10 percent.

2 The third, not examined in detail here, is food and beverages. Furthermore, the two-digit ISIC category for garments also includes footwear and leather products; in the discussion here, we leave those activities aside, focusing only on garments and textiles.

3 The discussion of this section draws on Arnold *et al.* (1994).

4 In knitting activities as well, enterprises in Botswana showed substantially more dynamism than the average for the sector: 36 percent of them grew, and less than 40 percent were classified as reflecting supply–push forces. As in other countries, however, there was little reliance on paid workers (only about 5 percent of the labor force). The sample size is small, however, accounting for less than 0.5 percent of all knitting enterprises in the six countries under study.

5 Specifically, once again a linear functional form was used to estimate a regression equation using ordinary least-squares estimation techniques. Dummy variables were used for the location, strata, gender, country, and sector variables. The sectoral categories were: woodworking, other forest-based manufacturing, forest-based trade, and grass, cane, and bamboo; knitting and weaving, dressmaking and tailoring, and other garments. The dependent variable was the annual average rate of increase since start-up. See McPherson (1995) for details.

6 These ideas are explored in more detail in Mead (1992).

7 For a fuller discussion of these alternatives and a review of a number of projects designed to use them for small-enterprise promotion, see Mead (1994a).

8 In the Dominican Republic, for example, only 15 percent of the employees of male-owned MSEs are women (Cely 1993).

9 Similar findings were earlier reported for MSEs in Egypt (Davies *et al.* 1992).

10 Such gender differences also occur at an even more disaggregate level. In their analysis of forest-based enterprises in Southern/Eastern Africa, for example, Arnold *et al.* (1994) report that the existing grass, cane, and bamboo enterprises, the majority of which were female owned, grew at an annual rate of 4 percent, while the woodworking enterprises, where virtually all the entrepreneurs were male, grew at an annual rate of 31 percent. Downing and Daniels (1992) also found that the slower growth rate for female-owned firms typically also held at the more disaggregate level within sectors.

11 Daniels (1995) also discovered that female-owned MSEs in Zimbabwe were more likely to expand their employment than were their male-owned counterparts. In addition, there was some initial evidence from Jamaica that by using employment rather than real sales measures of growth, one may be relatively understating the performance of female-owned MSEs (Gustafson and Liedholm 1995).

12 It should be noted, however, that a similar analysis undertaken with data from the Dominican Republic could find no statistical significance between ownership gender and growth (Cabal 1995).

5 MSEs and the macroeconomy

1 Labor force estimates are notoriously unreliable. For five countries in Africa covered by our surveys, the UNDP has estimated the growth of the labor force at 72 percent of the growth in population of working age (see Mead 1994a, for details). If the relationship holds in the Dominican Republic, it implies that the growth of employment in MSEs absorbed about 40 percent of the growth in the labor force in these six countries.

2 Many of jobs created through new start-ups will not endure. Since there is a significant attrition among newly established enterprises net employment creation through new start-ups (i.e. net of firms going out of business) is significantly less than the gross figure (i.e. employment in new start-ups, without taking account of job losses through the closure of previously existing firms). The figures in Table 5.2 are intermediate between gross and net figures. They excluded employment in MSEs that started and then closed in the past, but they include enterprises started in the past but that will close in the future. Since closure rates are highest in the first few years of an MSE's life, data on older cohorts are closer to being net estimates, while data for newer firms are closer to being gross estimates.

3 See Haggblade and Liedholm (1991) for a more detailed formulation of these arguments.

6 Problems faced by MSEs

1 The perceived problem question was not posed at different stages in the firm life cycle in the Dominican Republic; consequently, the Dominican Republic had to be excluded from the analysis. In the five core African countries, questions about problems in most cases were asked only of a sample of enterprises covered in the baseline survey. In these countries, this supplementary questionnaire was administered to 2,946 enterprises. In Malawi, a question about the most important problem faced at the time of the survey was included in the baseline survey; this means that, in that country, this question was asked of 9,600 enterprises.

2 In most of the tables of this chapter, average figures across countries are weighted averages using as weights the total number of small enterprises in the country. In four cases, the number of enterprises with data for that particular category was so small that this weighting procedure gave erratic and unrepresentative results. For example, in Table 6.5, among enterprises engaged in grass, cane, and bamboo activities, only two enterprises in Botswana fell into this category; using the full Botswana weight for these two enterprises gave highly misleading results. For those categories where the sum of responses in the four countries (Botswana, Kenya, Swaziland, and Zimbabwe) was less than 100, the individual responses across the four countries were summed and used to calculate the breakdown of problem types, without weighting by country. The resulting figure was then averaged with the breakdown for Malawi, which had a larger sample in each case (since the question was asked in the baseline questionnaire rather than the supplementary questionnaire), using the weighting system indicated at the start of this note. The four categories handled in this way were tailoring and dressmaking, cane and

bamboo, woodworking (all in Table 6.5), and enterprises that had graduated (in Table 7.3).

3 The main headings included under "other problems" in Kenya included personal problems (sickness etc.), problems resulting from inflation and devaluation, and problems with the premises (too little space etc.).

7 The diverse characteristics and needs of MSEs

1 The figures in this paragraph are derived from survey data in the six core countries: Botswana, Kenya, Malawi, Swaziland and Zimbabwe, and the Dominican Republic.

2 Kilby's (1988) review of the Kenya Industrial Estates program provides a clear statement of the dangers arising from a failure to heed this message. Kilby's analysis places the justification for such interventions in the context of a desire to "break the entrepreneurial bottleneck." He indicates that, in the face of limited numbers of enterprises in the 10–50 worker range and limited "graduation" into this category by smaller enterprises, major programs in several countries in Africa have attempted both to train potential entrepreneurs and to provide mechanisms whereby public sector institutions could supplement or even replace the limited capacities of private business people to undertake various entrepreneurial functions. His careful review of the Kenya effort, which leads him to judge it to be a failure for a long list of reasons, should be required reading for anyone considering the establishment of a program of this type.

8 Summary and implications

1 An exception is the recent survey of MSEs in Mozambique, which found that entrepreneurs that were members of business associations earned substantially and significantly higher incomes from their business than their neighbors who were not members; see Benfica (1998: 117).

Bibliography

Acs, Zoltan and David Audretsch (1989) "Births and Firm Size," *Southern Economic Journal*, vol. 56, no. 2.

Allison, P. D. (1984) "Event History Analysis: Regression for Longitudinal Event Data", Sage University Papers, Sage Publications, Beverly Hills, CA.

Anderson, Dennis (1982) "Small Industry in Developing Countries: A Discussion of Issues," *World Development*, vol. 10, no. 11, pp. 913–48.

Arnold, J. E. M., C. Liedholm, D. Mead, and I. M. Townson (1994) "Structure and Growth of Small Enterprises in the Forest Sector in Southern and Eastern Africa," Oxford Forestry Institute Occasional Papers No. 47, Oxford University, Oxford.

Arrighetti, Alesandro (1994) "Entry, Growth and Survival of Manufacturing Firms," *Small Business Economics*, vol. 6, pp. 127–37.

Banerji, Ranadev (1978) "Small-Scale Production Units in Manufacturing: An International Cross-Section Overview," *Weltwirtschaftsliches Archiv*, vol. 144, no. 1, pp. 62–84.

Benfica, R. M. S. (1998) "An Analysis of the Contribution of Micro and Small Enterprises to Rural Household Income in Central and Northern Mozambique," MS Thesis, Department of Agricultural Economics. Michigan State University.

Berger, Marguerite (1989) "Giving Women Credit: The Strength and Limitations of Credit as a Tool for Alleviating Poverty," *World Development*, vol. 17, no. 7 (July).

Berry, Albert and Armando Pinell-Siles (1979) "Small-Scale Enterprises in Colombia: A Case Study," World Bank Studies on Employment and Rural Development #56, Washington, DC.

Birch, David (1987) *Job Creation in America*, New York: The Free Press.

Boomgard, James, S. Davies, S. Haggblade, and D. C. Mead (1992) "A Subsector Approach to Small Enterprise Promotion and Research," *World Development*, vol. 20, No 2, pp. 199–212.

Brock, William and David Evans (1986) *The Economics of Small Business*, New York: Holmes & Meier.

Cabal, Miguel (1992) *Microempresas y Pequenas Empresas en la Republica Dominicana*, Resultados de una Encuesta Nacional. Fondo para el Financiamento de la

Microempresa, Inc. (FONDOMICRO), Santo Domingo, Dominican Republic, August.

Cabal, Miguel (1993) *Evolucion de las Microempresas y Pequenas Empresas en la Republica Dominicana, 1992–1993*, Fondo para el Financiamento de la Microempresa, Inc. (FONDOMICRO), Santo Domingo, Dominican Republic, June.

Cabal, Miguel (1995) "Growth, Appearances and Disappearances of Micro and Small Enterprises in the Dominican Republic," PhD Dissertation, Michigan State University.

Cely, Patricia (1993) *Microempresas y Pequenas Empresas de Mujeres* en la Republica Dominicana: Resultados de una Encuesta Nacional, Fondo para el Financiamento de la Microempresa, Inc. (FONDOMICRO), Santo Domingo, Dominican Republic, June.

Chuta, Enyinna (1990) "A Nigerian Study of Firm Dynamics," MSU International Development Working Paper No. 38.

Chuta, Enyinna and C. Liedholm (1985) *Employment and Growth in Small-Scale Industry: Empirical Evidence and Policy Assessment from Sierra Leone*, London: St Martins Press.

Cortes, Mariluz, A. Berry, and A. Ishaq (1987) *Success in Small and Medium-Scale Enterprises: The Evidence from Colombia*, A World Bank Research Publication, New York: Oxford University Press.

Daniels, Lisa (1994) "Changes in the Small-Scale Enterprise Sector from 1991 to 1993: Results of a Second Nationwide Survey in Zimbabwe," GEMINI Technical Report No. 71, March.

Daniels, Lisa (1995) "Entry and Exit Behavior and Growth Patterns among Small-Scale Enterprises in Zimbabwe," PhD Dissertation, Michigan State University.

Daniels, Lisa and Y. Fisseha (1992) "Micro- and Small-Scale Enterprises in Botswana: Results of a Nationwide Survey," GEMINI Technical Report No. 46, August.

Daniels, Lisa, D. C. Mead, and M. Musinga (1995) "Employment and Income in Micro and Small Scale Enterprises in Kenya: Results from a 1995 Survey," GEMINI Technical Report No. 92.

Daniels, Lisa and A. Ngwira (1993) "Results of a Nationwide Survey on Micro, Small and Medium Enterprises in Malawi," GEMINI Technical Report No. 53, January.

Davies, Stephen, D. C. Mead, and J. L. Seale (1992) "Small Manufacturing Enterprises in Egypt," *Economic Development and Cultural Change*, vol. 40, no. 2, January.

de Soto, Hernando (1989) *The Other Path*, New York: Harper & Row.

Downing, Jeanne (1990) "Gender and the Growth and Dynamics of Microenterprises," GEMINI Working Paper No. 5, October.

Downing, Jeanne and L. Daniels (1992) "The Growth and Dynamics of Women Entrepreneurs in Southern Africa," GEMINI Technical Report no. 47, August.

Dunne, Paul and Alan Hughes (1994) "Age, Size, Growth and Survival: UK Companies in the 1980s," *Journal of Industrial Economics*, vol. XI, no. 2, pp. 115–40.

Dunne, Timothy, Mark Roberts, and Larry Samuelson (1989) "The Growth and Failure of U.S. Manufacturing Plants," *Quarterly Journal of Economics*, November.

Evans, David (1987) "Test of Alternative Theories of Firm Growth," *Journal of Political Economy*, vol. 95, no. 4.

Fisseha, Yacob (1990) "Small Scale Enterprises in Niger: Survey Results from Dosso and Maradi Departments," Consultancy Report to USAID/Niger, March.

Fisseha, Yacob (1991) "Small-Scale Enterprises in Lesotho: Summary of a Country-wide Survey," GEMINI Technical Report No. 14, March.

Fisseha, Yacob (1994) "A Dynamic Study of Jamaican Micro and Small-Scale Enterprises," GEMINI Technical Report No. 70, March.

Fisseha, Yacob and M. A. McPherson (1991) "A Countrywide Study of Small-Scale Enterprises in Swaziland," GEMINI Technical Report No. 24, December.

Frischman, Alan (1988) "The Survival and Disappearance of Small Scale Enterprises in Urban Kano, 1973–1980," Draft paper.

Geroski, Paul (1991) *Market Dynamics and Entry*, Oxford: Blackwell.

Gibrat, R. (1931) *Les Inégalités Economiques*, Paris.

Grierson, John and D. C. Mead (1995) "Business Linkages in Zimbabwe: Concept, Practice, Strategies," GEMINI Working Paper No. 49.

Grierson, John, Donald C. Mead, and Sam Moyo (1997) "Business Linkages in Zimbabwe: Helping to Shape 'Win-Win' Economic Structures," *Development in Practice*, vol. 7, no. 3, pp. 304–7.

Gustafson, Todd and C. Liedholm (1995) "Patterns of Change Among Jamaican Microenterprises: Results from a Quarterly Panel Survey," GEMINI Technical Report No. 89, July.

Haggblade, Steve and P. Hazell (1989) "Agricultural Technology and Farm-Nonfarm Growth Linkages," *Agricultural Economics*, vol. 3, pp. 345–64.

Haggblade, Steve, P. Hazell, and J. Brown (1989) "Farm-Nonfarm Linkages in Rural Sub-Saharan Africa," *World Development*, vol. 17, no. 8, pp. 1173–1201.

Haggblade, Steve and C. Liedholm (1991) "Agriculture, Rural Labor Markets and the Evolution of the Rural Nonfarm Economy," GEMINI Working Paper No. 19.

Haggblade, Steve, C. Liedholm, and Donald Mead (1986) "The Effect of Policy and Policy Reforms on Non-Agricultural Enterprises in Developing Countries: A Review of Past Experiences," EEPA Discussion Paper No. 1, Cambridge, MA: Harvard Institute for International Development.

Haggblade, Steve and N. Ritchie (1991) "Opportunities for Intervention in Thailand's Silk Subsector," GEMINI Working Paper No. 26.

Hammermesh, Daniel (1993) *The Demand for Labor*, Princeton, NJ: Princeton University Press.

Hart, P. and S. J. Prais (1956) "The Analysis of Business Concentration: A Statistical Approach," *Journal of the Royal Statistical Society*, no. 119, part 2.

Ho, Sam (1980) *Small Scale Enterprises in Korea and Taiwan*, World Bank Staff Working Paper No. 384, Washington, DC: The World Bank.

Hoselitz, Bert F. (1959) "Small Industry in Under-Developed Countries," *Journal of Economic History*, vol. XIX, no. 4, pp. 600–18.

Ijiri, Y. and Herbert Simon (1977) *Skew Distributions and Size of Business Firms*, Amsterdam: North-Holland.

Johnston, Bruce and P. Kilby (1975) *Agriculture and Structural Transformation: Economic Strategies for Late-Developing Countries*, London: Oxford University Press.

Joumard, Isabelle, C. Liedholm, and D. C. Mead (1992) *The Impact of Laws and Regulations on Micro and Small Enterprises in Niger and Swaziland*, OECD Development Centre Technical Paper No. 77, Paris: Organization for Economic Cooperation and Development, September.

Jovanovic, B. (1982) "Selection and the Evolution of Industry," *Econometrica*, vol. 50, no. 3.

Kiefer, E. N. (1988) "Economic Duration Data and Hazard Functions," *Journal of Economic Literature*, June.

Kihlstrom, R. and J. J. Laffont (1979) "General Equilibrium Entrepreneurial Theory of Firm Formation Based on Risk Aversion," *Journal of Political Economy*, vol. 87, no. 4.

Kilby, Peter (1971) *Entrepreneurship and Economic Development*, New York: The Free Press.

Kilby, Peter (1988) "Breaking the Entrepreneurial Bottleneck in Late-Developing Countries: Is there a Useful Role for Government?" *Journal of Development Planning*, vol. 18, pp. 221–49.

Kilby, Peter (1994) "Nigeria, 1961–1991: Closure, Survival and Growth of Small Enterprises," Manuscript.

Leff, N. H. (1979) "Entrepreneurship and Development: The Problem Revisited," *Journal of Economic Literature*, March.

Liedholm, Carl (1990) "The Dynamics of Small-scale Industry in Africa and the Role of Policy," GEMINI Working Paper #2, Washington, DC.

Liedholm, Carl, and P. Kilby (1989) "The Role of Nonfarm Activities in the Rural Economy," *The Balance Between Industry and Agriculture in Economic Development*, ed. J. Williamson and V. Panchamuki, New York: St Martins Press.

Liedholm, Carl and M. A. McPherson (1991) "Small-Scale Enterprises in Mamelodi and Kwazakhele Townships South Africa: Survey Findings," GEMINI Technical Report No. 16, March.

Liedholm, Carl, M. McPherson, and E. Chuta (1994) "Small Enterprise Employment Growth in Rural Africa," *American Journal of Agricultural Economics*, December. pp. 1177–82.

Liedholm, Carl and D. C. Mead (1987) *Small Scale Industries in Developing Countries: Empirical Evidence and Policy Implications*, MSU International

Development Paper No. 9, East Lansing, MI: Department of Agricultural Economics, Michigan State University.

Liedholm, Carl and D. C. Mead (1991) "Dynamics of Microenterprises: Research Issues and Approaches," GEMINI Working Paper No. 12, January.

Liedholm, Carl and D. C. Mead (1993) "The Structure and Growth of Microenterprise in Southern and Eastern Africa: Evidence from Recent Surveys," GEMINI Working Paper No. 36, March.

Liedholm, Carl and D. C. Mead (1994) *Growth and Dynamics of Micro and Small Enterprises: A Comparative Analysis of Southern and Eastern Africa and Other Economies*, Manuscript.

Liedholm, Carl and J. Parker (1989) "Small Scale Manufacturing Growth in Africa: Initial Evidence," MSU International Development Working Paper No. 33, East Lansing MI: Department of Agricultural Economics, Michigan State University.

Little, Ian, D. Mazumdar, and J. Page (1987) *Small Manufacturing Enterprises: A Comparative Analysis of India and Other Economies*, A World Bank Research Publication, New York: Oxford University Press.

Lucas, R. E. (1978) "On the Size Distribution of Business Firms," *Bell Journal of Economics*, August.

McCormick, Dorthy and P. O. Pedersen, eds (1996) *Small Enterprises: Flexibility and Networking in an African Context*, Nairobi: Longhorn, Kenya.

McPherson, Michael A. (1991) "Micro and Small-Scale Enterprises in Zimbabwe: Results of a Country-wide Survey," GEMINI Technical Report No. 25, December.

McPherson, Michael A. (1992) "Growth and Survival of Small Southern African Firms", PhD Dissertation, Department of Economics, Michigan State University.

McPherson, Michael A. (1995) "Growth of Small Enterprises in Southern Africa," *Journal of Development Economics*, October.

McPherson, Michael A. and C. Henry (1994) "Rural Micro and Small Enterprises in Malawi: Effects of Burley Tobacco Policy Changes," Mimeographed report for USAID/Malawi.

McPherson, Michael and C. Liedholm (1996) "Determinants of Small and Micro Enterprise Registration: Results from Surveys in Niger and Swaziland," *World Development*. vol. 24, no. 3, pp. 481–7.

McPherson, Michael and Joan Parker (1993) "A Manual for Collecting Baseline Surveys of Micro and Small Scale Enterprises," GEMINI Field Research Study #1, Washington, DC.

Mata, Jose and Pedro Portugal (1994) "Life Duration of New Firms," *Journal of Industrial Economics*, vol. XLII, no. 3, pp. 227–45.

Mead, Donald C. (1992) "Microenterprise Development in a Subsector Context," *Small Enterprise Development*, vol. III, no. 1, pp. 35–42.

Mead, Donald C. (1994a) "The Contribution of Small Enterprises to Employment Growth in Southern and Eastern Africa," *World Development*, vol. 22, no. 12, pp. 1881–94.

Mead, Donald C. (1994b) "The Legal, Regulatory and Tax Framework and Small Enterprises," *Small Enterprise Development*, vol. V, no. 2, pp. 10–17.

Mead, Donald C., T. Dichter, Y. Fisseha, and S. Haggblade (1990) "Prospects for Enhancing the Performance of Micro- and Small-Scale Non-farm Enterprises in Niger," GEMINI Working Paper No. 3, February.

Mead, Donald C. and P. Kunjeku (1993) "Business Linkages and Enterprise Development in Zimbabwe," GEMINI Technical Report No. 55.

Mead, Donald C., H. Mukwenha, and L. Reed (1993) "Growth and Transformation Among Small Enterprises in Zimbabwe," Mimeographed paper.

Mellor, John (1976) *The New Economics of Growth*, Ithaca, NY: Cornell University Press.

Middleton, Alan (1989) "The Changing Structure of Petty Production in Ecuador," *World Development*, vol. 17, no. 1, pp. 139–55.

Nag, A. (1980) "Small Industries: Aspects of their Mortality," *The Economic Times*, October 6, Delhi, India.

Otero, Maria and E. Rhyne (1994) *The New World of Microenterprise Finance: Building Healthy Financial Institutions for the Poor*, West Hartford, CN: The Kumarian Press.

Page, John (1979) "Small Enterprises in African Development: A Survey," World Bank Staff Working Paper #363, Washington, DC.

Pakes, A. and R. Ericson (1987) "Empirical Implications of Alternative Models of Firm Dynamics," University of Wisconsin Social Science Systems Research Institute.

Parker, Joan (1994) "Patterns of Business Growth: Micro and Small Enterprises in Kenya," PhD Dissertation, Michigan State University.

Parker, Joan and C. Aleke Dondo (1991) "Kenya: Kibera's Small Enterprise Sector – Baseline Survey Report," GEMINI Working Paper No. 17, April.

Parker, Joan with T. Torres (1994) "Micro- and Small-Scale Enterprises in Kenya: Results of the 1993 National Baseline Survey," GEMINI Technical Report No. 75, March.

Parker, Ronald L., R. I. Riopelle, and W. F. Steel (1995) *Small Enterprises Adjusting to Liberalization in Five African Countries*, Washington, DC: World Bank Discussion Paper No. 271, Africa Technical Department Series.

Phillips, Bruce D. (1988) "Birth and Death Rates of Small and Large Firms: 1976–1986," Mimeographed paper.

Phillips, Bruce D. and Bruce A. Kirchhoff (1988) "Analysis of New Firm Survival and Growth," Paper presented at the Babson Entrepreneurship Research Conference, Calgary, Canada, May.

Piore, Michael J. and C. Sabel (1984) *The Second Industrial Divide*, New York: Basic Books.

Reardon, T., E. Crawford, and V. Kelly (1994) "Links Between Nonfarm Income and Farm Investment in African Households," *American Journal of Agricultural Economics*, December, 1172–6.

Schmitz, H. (1995) "Collective Efficiency: Growth Path for Small Scale Industry," *Journal of Development Studies*, vol. 31, no. 4, pp. 529–66.

Sherer, F. M. (1980) *Industrial Market Structure and Market Performance*, Boston: Houghton-Mifflin.

Simon, Herbert and Charles Bonini (1958) "The Size Distribution of Business Firms", *American Economic Review*, September.

Snodgrass, Donald and T. Biggs and Associates (1996) *Industrialization and the Small Firm: Patterns and Policies*, San Francisco: International Center for Economic Growth and Harvard Institute for International Development.

Steel, William F. and L. Webster (1990) *Small Enterprises in Ghana: Responses to Adjustment*, Industry and Energy Department Working Paper, Industry Series Paper No. 33, Washington, DC: The World Bank, September.

Swain, Frank and Bruce Phillips (1985) "The Relationship Between Business Failures and Economic Growth: 1978–1984," Mimeographed paper, Office of Advocacy, US Small Business Administration, Washington, DC, September.

Swaziland, Central Statistical Office (1990) *Annual Statistical Bulletin, 1989*, Mbabane.

Timberg, Tom (1978) "Report on the Survey of Small Scale Industry Units in Bombay," Washington, DC: The World Bank.

TIPCO (The Information Processing Company) (no date) "Periphery Trade and Enterprise Development Study," Consultancy Report for USAID (mimeo).

UNDP and The World Bank (1992) *African Development Indicators*, Washington, DC: The World Bank.

United States Agency for International Development (1994) *Strategies for Sustainable Development*, Washington, DC: USAID (March).

Van Dijk, Meine Peter and R. Rabellotti, editors (1997) *Enterprise Clusters and Networks in Developing Countries*, London: Frank Cass, EADI Book Series 20.

Wagner, Joachiem (1994) "The Post-Entry Performance of New Small Firms in German Manufacturing Industries," *Journal of Industrial Economics*, vol. XLII, no. 2, pp. 141–54.

Weidemann, C. Jean (1992) "Egyptian Women and Microenterprise: The Invisible Entrepreneurs," GEMINI Technical Report No. 34, March.

Wierda, David (1994) "Micro and Small Enterprises in the Prefecture of Labe, Guinea," Aide au Developpement, CRWRC-Guinea.

World Bank (1989) *Sub-Saharan Africa: From Crisis to Sustainable Growth: A Long-term Perspective Study*, Washington, DC: The World Bank.

World Bank (1993) *World Development Report, 1993*, New York: Oxford University Press.

Zimbabwe Central Statistical Office (1992) *Quarterly Digest of Statistics*, Harare, September.

Index